The COMPLETE BOOK of CLOSING SALES

The COMPLETE BOOK of CLOSING SALES

Sal T. Massimino

A DIVISION OF AMERICAN MANAGEMENT ASSOCIATIONS

Library of Congress Cataloging in Publication Data

Massimino, Sal T.
  The complete book of closing sales.

  Includes index.
  1. Selling. 2. Sales management. I. Title.
HF5438.25.M374   658.1'1   80-69684
ISBN 0-8144-5592-1   AACR2

© 1981 AMACOM
A division of American Management Associations, New York. All rights reserved. Printed in the United States of America.

This publication may not be reproduced, stored in a retrieval system, or transmitted in whole or in part, in any form or by any means, electronic, mechanical, photocopying, recording, or otherwise, without the prior written permission of AMACOM, 135 West 50th Street, New York, N.Y. 10020.

First Printing

Contents

INTRODUCTION 1

SECTION I: FACTS THAT HELP YOU CLOSE SALES

1: *Listening to the Buyer*	9
2: *Ways to Hold the Buyer's Attention*	24
3: *Using Product Options to Close*	36
4: *Price Negotiations*	44
5: *Giving Something for Nothing*	53
6: *Nonstop Selling*	59
7: *Follow-up Selling*	69

SECTION II: THE SALES MANAGER'S ROLE IN CLOSING

8: *Training Salespeople to Close*	77
9: *Teaching to Close by Example*	99
10: *What to Do with the Salesperson Who Can't Close*	105

SECTION III: 250 SUCCESSFUL CLOSING LINES

11: *Fifty Closing Lines That Work in Retail Selling*	115
12: *Fifty Closing Lines That Work in Industrial Selling*	118

*13: Fifty Closing Lines That Work in Wholesale
    Sales*   122
*14: Fifty Closing Lines That Work When Selling
    Intangibles*   125
*15: Fifty Closing Lines That Work When Selling
    Internationally*   129

APPENDIX A: SOME TYPICAL SALES LETTERS THAT
HELP YOU CLOSE SALES   133

APPENDIX B: SOME TYPICAL FOLLOW-UP SALES
LETTERS AIMED AT CLOSING   139

INDEX   147

Introduction

Until a sale is closed, no other steps in the selling process have meaning. No matter how good you are at prospecting, making presentations, and wining and dining clients, everything is wasted unless you close the sale. It doesn't matter at all that prospects say, "He's a great guy," or "She's always pleasant." Selling is not a popularity contest—although it's easier to close sales if your prospects find you personable. Selling *is* closing— getting a yes whether the original answer was no or maybe. Without closing, there is no sale.

In my many years of selling and managing salespeople, I have found that closing is the weakest area for most people. This was the first area I mastered—with much hard work. The least-used, the most important, and perhaps the easiest technique is to ask for the business—again and again if necessary. Yet even experienced salespeople often forget to ask for the order. Over the years, I have continued to perfect as many types of closing approaches as possible. In managing my own sales staffs, I have taught these methods repeatedly. They are easy to learn. You can put them to work at once to double or triple your present sales volume.

This book was written to help you learn the fine art of closing sales. It is divided into three parts to enable you to quickly find the information that most directly applies to you. In the first section, you will find facts to help you close sales. These seven chapters will be essential if you are a salesperson and will remind you of the many good ways to close if you are a sales manager. Especially important is Chapter 1, which explains how to listen to prospects and buyers to find out what you can sell them and how much, as well as when and how to close the sale. Ways to hold the buyer's attention, the use of product options to close, and price negotiations that help you close are all covered in this section, too. Practical, time-tested methods, drawn from every type of selling, are discussed in these chapters.

Give-to-get selling is discussed in Chapter 5. With this method, the buyer gets something for nothing, to help you close. The "something" may be a service already offered by your firm, one that won't take even an extra minute of your time, except the time to offer it to the prospect.

Chapter 6 is about nonstop selling, a technique every salesperson should know but obviously does not. Persistence is the key to many sales, and this chapter tells you how to be persistent without being obnoxious.

Follow-up selling techniques are given in Chapter 7. If you've ever lost a sale because the buyer changed his or her mind once you'd left, you will be eager to learn these methods of making sure a closed sale stays closed.

Section II contains all the information a sales manager will need to train salespeople to close, and to motivate and manage salespeople once that training is complete. Whether you're a sales manager now or would like to be one in the future, this section is for you. Chapter 8 gives training methods, describing step by step how to set up and operate a training program that effectively teaches salespeople in any field to close their sales.

One example may be worth thousands of words, and Chapter 9 shows you how to teach your sales staff to close by example.

Chapter 10 tells you how to deal with salespeople who appear to have potential but can't seem to learn the basic closing techniques. Field-tested methods that have been successful with

Introduction

the most difficult salespeople, trainees and experienced staff alike, are provided in this key chapter.

Section III provides 250 of the most important sentences you as a salesperson will ever read. The section contains 50 successful closing lines each for retail selling, industrial selling, wholesale sales, selling intangibles, and selling internationally. Whether you memorize the lines that apply to your own area of sales or decide to use variations, the closing line will be the final touch that can help you double or triple your sales.

SELLING IS AN ART

How is it possible to put the art of selling on paper? Selling cannot be turned into a formula, although some companies try to do this. A sales pitch that a salesperson has been required to memorize will sound like what it is—a canned speech learned by rote. It won't work.

What *can* be put on paper, and what I have put into this book, are the keys to closing. Read, consider, and reread the information about these methods. Let the techniques sink into your mind, your approach to a client, and your everyday selling attitude. Adapt them when necessary, as I have done in many of the examples. Use them exactly when they fit. Create new methods from the techniques given here, for unique closing situations.

Part of the art of selling and closing is letting yourself feel what is going on around you. Think back to your last sale. Do you remember your personal manner, your moves—getting up to tower over a sitting prospective client when you wanted to impress him or her, looking the prospect straight in the eyes— your feeling of enthusiasm, the exhilaration of realizing that the client is giving signals that he or she is ready for you to close? If not, it is important that you test your memory of what happened during a sales call after you have made it. Let yourself mentally see and feel each detail of the presentation and close. This will tell you what is good and bad about your selling and will let you know which areas of this book are most important for making positive additions to your selling and closing techniques.

Another part of the art of selling and closing is knowing your product and service better than anyone else does. You will never be able to sell well unless you do—even with the best closing lines in the world.

Part of the art of selling is also being sure that you know the basics. Is the term *basics* too demeaning for you if you are an experienced salesperson? Don't let it be. Basics change, just as time passes. Methods that worked a year or two ago may not be as effective today. Closing techniques that worked three or four years ago may not be sophisticated enough for today's buyer.

This book will bring you up to date on what works now when selling and closing your sales.

A Con Artist Is Not a Salesperson

One of the most important things to learn in closing sales is that intimidating customers to get them to buy something is a bad way to sell. If you use this tactic, you are a con artist but not a salesperson.

My personal theory has always been that I have never *sold* anything in my life. Instead, I show a prospective buyer that I have something that he or she needs. The prospect buys this need from me.

My own selling history shows how and why this philosophy works. Before entering sales, I was an accountant. What a let-down from the career I expected! I counted other people's money, kept track of their income, and worked on their tax problems. In many cases, the tax problems amounted to more than my salary and potential earnings. But being an accountant did stress the importance of ethics to me.

Introduction

My first sales job was selling coin-operated radio services to managers of fifth-rate hotels in New York City. Later, I sold products, retail and wholesale, including such items as windshields, insurance, tax services, advertising space, and franchises. Many times, conning a prospect might have been the easiest way to make a single sale. But the con artist cannot make repeat sales. I was interested, as you should be, in selling as a profession.

SELLING IS SELLING

Selling is selling, even though closing is not always successfully closing. Competent salespeople can sell any kind of product or service, I believe, so long as they apply the proven professional methods of selling and closing.

Everything you will need to know to close sales is included in this volume. Use it well, with my wishes for a lifetime of successful closing.

I

FACTS that HELP YOU CLOSE SALES

Closing sales regularly depends on using tested methods. Many salespeople develop some good closing methods by chance, but there is no reason to rely on luck to help you close.
In the following seven chapters, in which I address primarily the salesperson, I have presented what I consider the basic and essential steps needed to close sales. These include listening to the buyer, holding the buyer's attention, using product options, price negotiations, give-to-get selling, nonstop selling, and follow-up selling. If you learn and regularly use these basic keys to selling, your closing record will soar.

1

Listening to the buyer

If you listen carefully to the buyer, you will be able to close with much greater ease. Your ears can guide you to what your buyer wants and help you decide which parts of your sales presentation will be most useful. This sounds relatively simple, doesn't it?

It is not so simple to do, however, if you have been taught that salespeople must give their side of the story, including statistics, in order to sell. Forget sales training of this type, and instead, begin to listen.

GET THE PROSPECT TO TALK

Before you can listen for key facts to help you close a sale, the buyer must be persuaded to talk. Some prospects will start talking on their own, but many will not. When they don't, you must ask questions to get the information you need. Questions should be tailored to probable buyer needs, yet they should be general enough to encourage all types of buyers.

For example, if you are selling cars, you may want to ask questions that will tell you how the buyer plans to use the automobile. "Do you use your car in your line of work?" will often evoke an answer that tells you what kind of car is needed.

"No, I take the train to work and my wife uses the car to haul the kids around" may be one answer. Listening to this reply tells you that it might be wise to suggest a four-door model or a station wagon, for easier access.

Or the prospect may reply, "I sure do—seems like I always have more clients to entertain." Listening to this reply again signals the need for a four-door model, so that the buyer's clients will find it easy to get in and out of the car.

If you are selling a product less tangible than an automobile, ask appropriate questions. For example, when selling a business franchise, ask questions that will tell you the reasons the buyers are considering a business operation. A general question such as "Do you plan to operate the business yourself?" is a good opener. Listening to the answer will tell you whether the prospects are buying for themselves or whether their purchase is an investment that will be run by a manager.

Keep alert for replies that tell you personal, emotional reasons that may help you the most when closing. "My husband thinks it would keep me busy and provide good job insurance for him," the wife of a buying couple may remark in a very casual tone. Such an answer is anything but casual. If you were listening, you learned that the wife is probably bored and looking for a new or renewed career. You also heard that the husband is probably either unhappy or insecure in his own job and wants a source of income if something goes wrong with his job. These insights will help you present those aspects of your product or service that will later help you close the sale.

Whatever your product or service, be sure to talk your prospect's language when you ask questions. Don't phrase your questions in technical jargon, for instance, unless you know for certain that the buyer is completely comfortable with it. If you're selling a boat, stick to questions about the prospect's potential use and needs for a boat; don't talk about engine parts unless you're sure the buyer has an extensive mechanical background.

Ask personal questions, within the bounds of good taste. "Do you like that shade of blue?" a dress shop salesperson may ask.

"No, I don't like blue at all. Green is my color," may come the reply. If the salesperson has listened, she will suggest green garments that are good styles for the prospect.

A bit more touchy, but very necessary to close, is determining who makes the decision in a couple or other buying group. "Will you both be operating the business?" the franchise seller may ask a couple. Listen first to see who answers, and consider the content of the answer second.

"No, my wife will operate the business, at least to start," the husband may reply. Since the husband answered, the salesperson can assume that the main decision will be made by him and that he will provide or arrange for the needed financing.

This doesn't mean that the salesperson should ignore the wife, who also needs to be "closed." It does mean that the sales presentation should be made to meet the husband's needs—investment return, job insurance, and so on—first.

Not every salesperson knows how to listen to answers. For instance, when you ask a question, the prospect will usually do more than answer that question. He or she will talk about other subjects, too. Don't stop listening once your questions are answered. Listen and you may learn details about the prospect's (or his or her company's) financial situation, labor problems, and many other factors that can help you close future sales.

For example, an advertising manager complained about the recession to one of the advertising space reps working for me. This complaint had nothing to do with questions the salesman had asked his prospect. The fact that the salesman listened, however, had a great deal to do with closing the sale.

"You're right about the effect of the recession on domestic sales," the salesman told the buyer. "That's why it's so important to concentrate your advertising in the international magazines that reach markets that are still strong. And with the U.S. dollar as depleted as it is today, you should be very competitive in the international marketplace."

Figure 1. Use both sides of a standard 5" by 8" card to record important client facts gleaned from listening to your customers. The information will help you close future as well as current sales.

CLIENT				PRODUCTION		
FIRM				AGENCY		
ADDRESS				ADDRESS		
		POST CODE				POST CODE
PHONE		TELEX		PHONE		TELEX
NAMES		TITLE		NAME		TITLE
			P.A.L.			
PRODUCTS				SCHEDULE DATE:		

	JAN	FEB	MAR	APR	MAY	JUNE	JULY	AUG	SEPT	OCT	NOV	DEC

DATE	ISSUE	SIZE	COL.	PUBLICATION	COST

Put What You Hear on Paper

The best salespeople not only listen but record the most important information on customer record cards (see Figure 1), to help close future sales.

"We're really interested in selling to Africa right now," the advertising manager of a large equipment manufacturer may tell the advertising space salesperson. If this fact is recorded rather than heard and forgotten, the salesperson can use it on later sales calls. "Are you still interested in the African market?" he or she may begin. If the answer is yes, an increase in African circulation or publication coverage of Africa can be used to help close another sale.

Recording such information shows the salesperson's concern about his or her customers. For example, the owner of a dress shop made a customer card note that the new buyer was a size 6, disliked low necklines, and favored blues and greens. About two months after the initial sale, she called the customer. "We're having a special sale, and there are a number of small-sized garments in blue and green," she told the buyer. "I thought you might like to take a look." When the customer returned, you can be sure there were no low-necked garments among those shown.

Transferring what you hear to paper serves many purposes. Customer records can remind you of cyclical or seasonal buying patterns, for instance. A customer may purchase clothing regularly each spring or fall. The prospect may comment that he or she will buy a specific product in the summer, when there are no heating bills, or early in the year when a royalty check arrives. Such a comment may be an excuse not to buy, but it may also be the truth. If so, the salesperson who has listened and recorded the comment will be reminded to approach the buyer at the right time to close the sale.

Another good way to reinforce your listening once you're away from the buyer's desk or home is to make a sales priority chart (see Figure 2). Simply list the needs and wants as ex-

Listening to the Buyer 15

• *from the desk of* **SAL MASSIMINO**

```
              Sales Priority Chart

John Smith's wants/needs re:  Color TV

    1. Set size that fits 12-in.-tall by 14-in.-wide space.

    2. Reliable controls/color.

    3. Fair price.
```

Technical Publishing
a company of
The Dun & Bradstreet Corporation

Figure 2. A quickly written sales priority chart, made up of information the prospect has told you about wants and needs, can later be used to close the same.

pressed by the prospect, with the most important items first. This will help you zero in on the most important points when you make a follow-up call to close the sale. Information obtained from listening should always be used when preparing for subsequent sales calls.

The sales priority chart can also be used in telephone selling. For example, if a product or service has been advertised in a newspaper, the first contact with the prospect is often by telephone. In this case, keep a pad of paper by the phone and take notes on the wants and needs expressed. After the call is completed, arrange these needs in order of importance.

When selling investment property or other items where the first contact is usually by telephone, the salesperson often follows up the call by sending information. If this approach is used, it is essential that no sales pitch be included in the material sent, except in very subtle or indirect ways. For instance, the package may discuss other buyers and their satisfaction with the property as an investment, in addition to providing full details about the property itself.

Follow-up to this package may be by telephone or in person. In either case, the use of suitable questions and good listening are important.

Sell Yourself while You Listen

There is more to the art of sales listening than picking up clues about the buyer's needs, especially during early sales calls. No one likes to buy from a stranger, and no one will buy from a salesperson he or she doesn't trust. It is important, then, to use your questioning and listening skills to sell yourself. This does not mean that you should tell the buyer how wonderful and reliable you are. It does mean that you should:

○ Ask questions that show your concern about the buyer's wants

Listening to the Buyer

and needs. There is still no substitute for putting yourself in the buyer's place when selling.
- Compliment the prospect, using honest remarks, such as "I admire your knowledge of my product." This will help you get acquainted and make you less of a stranger.
- Know your product or service thoroughly and be able to answer questions; listen for clues to buyer needs.
- Be positive, smile, and show self-confidence in your conversation. This, too, will help you get acquainted faster.
- Be sincere in listening to the buyer's needs and in acting on them.
- Never disagree with a prospect; instead turn disagreements into problem solutions.
- Use the word *you* as often as possible when talking to the prospect.
- Ask your prospect's opinion; it will help you get acquainted and also provide information.
- Call your prospect by name, to get acquainted more quickly. People enjoy being addressed by name.
- Talk about subjects, including aspects of your product or service, that interest the prospect.

TELEPHONE LISTENING

It is very important to be a good listener when making sales calls on the telephone. Picking up clues is harder because you can't watch the prospect's face and body movements for feedback about his or her reaction.

Have a reason for calling. This might be to inquire whether the prospect has received a sample, market research data, or other materials you have sent. Ask for his or her opinion of the material or if he or she found it useful. Then listen to the reply, noting voice inflection and other clues to the buyer's wants and needs.

Remind the prospect of conversation from calls made in person. For example, you might say, "You mentioned last week that you'd be in a position to decide after a few days. Will we be able to help you with our XYZ product?"

Listen carefully, not only for clues to close, but also for indications that another personal call is needed. Don't forget to record important information on your customer record cards.

Adapting Your Presentation to What You Hear

Listening, whether in person or on the telephone, should guide your sales presentation. The word *sales* has a bad connotation for many prospects. They are afraid of being conned or coerced. For this reason, your buyer may ask for details about your products or services when such facts are the last thing that will help you close the sale. What is really needed are details about how your product or service can help the buyer. It is up to you to listen carefully enough to recognize nonproductive requests for facts and then turn the conversation to the buyer's wants and needs. By doing this, you will also be able to overcome the prospect's fear of salespeople.

How can presentations be adapted for listening? A good example is provided by an appliance salesman who had a couple looking at color television sets. As he listened, it became obvious that they were looking for a set to fit a small space. Only one set in the salesman's stock would fit the measurements. He then adapted his sales presentation to that one set, dropping his usual pitch about the advantages of large-screen sets and assuring the prospects that this set had many quality features even though it was small.

Listening on Your Own Turf

Sometimes the best listening—and selling—can be done on your own turf. Many prospects are flattered by an invitation to visit your factory or service organization. On your ground, you can freely show the advantages of your product or service, ask questions, and listen to the buyers with great care. Best of all, you can be sure the buyer will not be interrupted by telephone calls, business associates, and so on. In the case of potential large-volume sales, it can pay to reimburse the prospect—after he or she buys—for part of the travel expenses required to visit your operation. You'll be paying for a chance at uninterrupted listening.

Using Notes and Note Pads

Concentrate on what your prospect says. Make notes as soon as possible after you have left the prospect, to prevent forgetting important parts of the conversation. Some notes can be made during a conversation, because it shows that you are paying attention to what the prospect says. It makes the prospect feel important.

A simple piece of paper can help you in other ways, too. For example, you can prepare a small note pad before you call on your prospect; write the prospect's name at the top and follow this by a key question (see Figure 3). During the call, bring this pad from your briefcase. This will show the prospect that you have taken a few minutes to think about his or her own needs and problems. It also allows you to begin the questioning sequence and to practice listening. Be sure, however, to always use handwritten notes. If the presentation is too slick, it can turn a prospect off.

Listening to Change Negative Decisions

It is possible to turn negative buying decisions into positive closings. The secret is to listen to the prospect until a dead end or negative area begins to dominate the conversation. For example, if a prospect begins to talk about his or her budget being exhausted to one of the space sales representatives on my staff,

Figure 3. A simple note pad with the prospect's name and a key question—handwritten—can help you start the questioning and listening process.

that sales rep doesn't continue to listen quietly, nor does he or she give up and forget about closing the sale. Instead, the rep tries to relate back to something discussed on a previous call—marketplace potential, for example. He or she might confirm the prospect's choice of marketplaces and then suggest a few new geographical areas that would be worthwhile. The idea is to get the prospect to talk about positive areas so that you can listen and find ways to turn the information into a sale.

As the prospect talks and you listen, think about ways to overcome problems that have been raised. If the advertising budget is exhausted, for example, my advertising salespeople often suggest using funds originally budgeted for other areas of promotion, such as exhibitions, to advertise in a special issue or a special feature section.

If the account is not a new one, check sales records before you make a call. If frequency or volume discounts are given by your company, the buyer may be entitled to a lower price if he or she makes even one more purchase.

Ask about results and degree of satisfaction with previous purchases. If the reaction is favorable, you have a good starting point for making more sales. If the response is negative, you will want to help solve whatever problem the buyer encountered so that you can close future sales.

Listen, Then Give

One of the best ways listening can help close sales is to listen to the prospect's needs and then give him or her any ideas you have that can help meet those needs, whether or not those ideas are directly related to what you are selling.

As an outsider, you often have fresh views on problems that the prospect has struggled with until he or she can no longer see them clearly. For example, if you have an idea for promoting or publicizing the prospect's product or service, tell the prospect about it—even if you are selling office supplies. Buyers like salespeople who take a genuine interest in their needs. If you listen to learn those needs and then show a real interest, it will be much simpler to close sales.

GET THE LISTENING HABIT

To be able to listen properly when selling, it is necessary to get the listening habit. The only way to make listening a habit, of course, is to make it a major part of each day. You can help do this by consciously practicing good listening and by observing listening habits in others.

For example, if you ask your secretary for a particular paper, first be sure to give complete information about the materials you want. Then watch and see what happens. Does your secretary find the paper in your files and return it? Or is the wrong paper brought to you because of poor listening?

When you make your next sales call, notice how carefully the receptionist listens. Does he or she ask for your business card, the spelling of your name, or whether you have an appointment? After you have provided such information, is it correctly relayed to your prospect?

In a restaurant, observe that a good waiter or waitress listens carefully and either writes down or remembers each order correctly. Less effective waiters and waitresses often do not remember the order or which person has ordered a specific dish.

You can practice your own listening habits every day by listening first of all to the names of people you meet—whether they are prospects or not. Repeat the name aloud to help you remember it, being sure to pronounce it correctly. Ask if the name has any special meaning. If it does, try to remember the name by tying it to a mental image of its meaning.

Listening exercises are easy, and they can be adapted to your own needs. Listen to every sound around you during the day, and especially listen to prospect and clients when you are selling. Let your prospects tell you how much they need what you have to offer. Then use this information to help you close your sales. Research studies show that on the average, we listen at a 25 percent efficiency level; that is, we assimilate only one quarter of what we hear. Imagine how much better you could close sales if you increased this level to 50 percent: You can, with practice.

2

Ways to hold the buyer's attention

To successfully close a sale, it is necessary to have the prospect's complete attention. A person will not buy your product or service if he or she is thinking about personal problems rather than concentrating on your sales presentation. The ability to grab the buyer's attention is as important as the ability to listen in closing sales.

Do Gimmicks Hold the Buyer's Attention?

Many salespeople rely on gimmicks to hold the buyer's attention. I've heard of salespeople who bring doughnuts or muffins to an early morning call. One salesman lays out a 100-foot-long presentation on the floor and has the client follow him around, looking at various graphic elements within the presentation, while the salesman makes explanations.

Gimmicks are a dime a dozen, and usually they don't work. Are you trying to razzle-dazzle your clients with a spectacular, or are you trying to convince them that your product or service is needed? If you want to razzle-dazzle prospects, do a tap dance, bring in a vaudeville group, hire an elephant, or whatever. Yes, you will hold their attention; but you may not hold their *buying* attention.

A perfect example of the use of gimmicks, and its ineffectiveness, can be seen at almost any trade show. A major manufacturer at a construction exhibition, for example, had an hourly show that consisted of three scantily clad girls dancing and singing, using a piece of the manufacturer's equipment as a stage. Each show drew large crowds of men within the industry. After the show, when questioned by a local newspaper reporter, these men remembered the girls and their act, but most could not name the manufacturer who used the gimmick.

At a mining show held some years ago, a truck manufacturer used a gimmick to demonstrate the exceptionally large size of the truck body. The truck body was filled with water, on the water was a small sailboat, and inside the sailboat was a girl in a bikini. At the onset of the next show, a magazine editor asked registrants if they remembered the exhibit from the display. "Oh, yes," was a common reply. "The girl in the boat in the truck—that was really something." But not one person of the 30 or more industry buyers interviewed could remember the manufacturer of the truck.

This is not to say that gimmicks don't work in some cases. But when you use a gimmick, you must also remember your goal!

When do gimmicks work? Their best value is probably in specialty selling, when the gimmick can be tied to the product or service to be sold. For example, a banana distributor used a chimpanzee act at a trade show. In the buyer's mind, it was easy to remember that the cute antics of the chimpanzee were related to bananas.

What Does Hold Attention?

Letting the prospect know how well you understand his or her problems, needs, and so on is the most basic way of holding his or her attention. Emphasize the ways in which the two of you are alike. Make the point that you both are really working for the same goal—generally, an improvement in the prospect's business or life (which will also improve your sales). State plainly that this similarity allows you to better help the prospect with needs and problems, no matter what the industry.

Realize what you are doing with this type of approach. You are relating to the prospect. You are holding your buyer's attention by identifying yourself with him or her. Once this is accomplished, in your prospect's eyes you are no longer the peddler who is trying to make a sale or a kill, you are just like him or her—earning a living and trying to help your customer along the way.

Sell satisfaction rather than the product or service. If your presentation is concentrated on the satisfactions the buyer will receive, you'll be sure to hold his or her attention.

Get the prospect involved. Put your imagination to work to think up ways of doing this. Using a handwritten message on a note pad is one method of involving a prospect in your presentation. Prepared written materials that start with a short test about information the buyer wants to know and end with answers can also be used effectively. Or hand prospects a sample, a pamphlet, or a new study about your product. Once their hands touch your materials, they are involved and will be more easily reached.

Keep an order pad in plain sight long before you need to use it. The prospect will feel involved with it and is less likely to be frightened off when you later begin to fill in the order details.

Frequent and appropriate use of the word *you* also helps involve the prospect in your presentation.

Make the product hard to get; keep it easy to buy. Many prospects become more involved when they are told a product is in scarce supply, one of a kind, a bargain since it's a prototype, and so on. Use these facts to hold the prospect's attention whenever possible.

A men's clothing salesman sold an expensive imported overcoat by telling his prospect, "It's the only one of this brand I'll be able to get this season." The buyer, who had not intended to buy an overcoat at all, got interested in the product—the style, the fabric, its uniqueness.

"It may not fit," the salesman continued. "But since it's the only one, why not try it on?"

The customer was involved. He tried on the coat, liked it, and was very pleased with his "rare" purchase.

At the same time, it is important that you hold the buyer's attention by making the product or service easy to buy. Budget payments, credit cards, late billing, and hard facts that show how a product or service can save the buyer money are all attention-getters that make it easy for him or her to buy. My sales staff, for example, carry comparative price charts listing brand name prices where our products have the price advantage.

Keep the presentation human. Testimonials, anecdotes, handwritten letters from satisfied customers—these will help you hold the buyer's attention as you move toward the sale's close.

Use imagination to hold the buyer's attention. In a presentation to the sales staff, the author of a management book on hiring held up a sign with the number 1,012. This is the average number of hiring interviews the manager conducts in a lifetime; the book, the author claimed, could help cut the number of interviews to a tenth of that figure. By showing the number first, the author captured his audience's attention.

Dealing with Business Interruptions

Getting the prospect's attention and keeping it are two different things, particularly if you are doing your selling at the buyer's place of business. In an office, a telephone call or another worker can easily interrupt your presentation.

For example, your prospect may have asked his or her secretary to hold all telephone calls. But, if the secretary leaves to do an errand and the telephone rings, your prospect will undoubtedly answer the phone. This breaks the span of attention the prospect has given to you and your product or service. This interruption can be drastic when you have brought your client's attention to the point that he or she is relating to you and beginning to understand what you have to offer.

What can you do after your prospect has completed the telephone call? First, remember that he or she may be angry because the secretary did not handle the call. The prospect might also be angry because he or she did not want to talk to the person who called or for other reasons concerning the content of the call. Even without any anger, the call will have put your presentation picture out of focus.

When the call is completed, you must quickly and very briefly recap the material you have already presented. This is necessary to bring your prospect back to the level of understanding prior to the interruption. Re-create the mental picture your prospect had of your products and services before the telephone disrupted the train of thought. Try to imagine yourself in your prospect's place, and say those things that will recall the points made earlier in the presentation. You and only you can put the pieces of your presentation together again. If you fail to bring the prospect back to the point of interruption, you will have lost all the precious time and effort you have already put into the sales call.

Usually, you will be able to restore your presentation to the point of the interruption—with one important exception. If your presentation has been interrupted at the actual close, you will probably not be able to bring the buyer's attention back to the selling point. In such a case, it may be better to find a polite way to end the meeting and return to close on another day.

If you find that you are regularly interrupted with a specific prospect, it is wise to make lunch dates rather than confining your calls to an office or home location. At lunch, you will be interrupted only by a waiter or waitress. Such interference can be controlled by you as the host.

Product Interest Can Help Hold Attention

You can hold a prospect's attention with nothing but product information and have enough attention to close the sale.

To begin, be sure that the prospective buyer knows the basic facts about your company, your product, your service, and yourself. If this is your first call, describe your company briefly, including details about its methods of operation and its background. Let the buyer know your firm is reputable and reliable, particularly if you are selling a new product or service that has not been "proven" on its own.

Very quickly, let the prospect know that you have researched his or her need for your product or service, and tell how you believe you can help meet those needs. Remember to keep each part of your presentation brief, relating product explanations to the buyer's needs and wishes.

Let the current economic conditions play a part in creating product interest. If you have done your homework, you will have all the facts and figures you need to show a prospect how your product is economical, whether because of lower cost or greater productivity. If the cost is the same as that of competitive products or services, you should be able to tell the buyer about some service you offer that your competitors do not.

Ask the prospect questions about your product or service that will result in affirmative answers. For example, you might ask if the buyer has owned similar products in the past or if he or she would like to save 10 percent on your product (assuming you have a sale or are 10 percent cheaper than your competitor). Affirmative answers mean that the prospect is agreeing with you. If the buyer agrees with you about product information, you will almost surely be able to close the sale.

Be careful to avoid any sort of debate as a means of holding the buyer's attention. Controversy may hold attention, but it will ruin your chances for a sale. No matter how much you try to prevent it, there will always be times when the prospect will disagree with you. Control your own anger and change the subject as quickly and smoothly as possible. If you read the local newspaper the day of the call, as I do, you may be able to turn the topic of conversation to some local issue as a means of avoiding a discussion of some national or personal conflict that can affect your sale. By turning to a local issue, the client will feel that you are interested in the same things he or she is and will become comfortable with you because of your interest.

The best ways to hold attention are the little touches—those that take less time than reading this chapter. Almost all of them center around showing a genuine interest in your client's needs and in how your product or service can help fill those needs.

USE ATTRACTIVE PRICING TO HOLD ATTENTION

Another sure way of holding the prospect's attention is to begin to talk about attractive prices for products or services he or she needs. This does not mean that you must always have the lowest prices but that you should always show a concern for the prospect's pocket. For example, if you can provide a discount on a specified volume of goods, be sure that your prospect knows this. If you can provide free training or marketing services, talk about them when you are making the initial presentation, so that your buyer knows he or she is getting something extra for the purchase price.

A good example of this can be seen with a sale made by one of my advertising space representatives. The salesman called on a drill manufacturer and was trying to persuade the manufacturer to place an advertisement in an upcoming magazine featuring a section on drilling. The manufacturer was mildly interested but had not allowed for such an advertisement in the budget.

"I believe that I can obtain a position for you—at no extra

cost—opposite the opening of the drilling feature," the space rep told the manufacturer. "Let me call the home office to check."

"That would be a good position," the prospect agreed.

The call was placed to me from the prospect's office. The position was still open, and I O.K.'d the offer. Within seconds, the sale was closed.

The same principle can be applied to other aspects of selling. You may not be able to give the prospect a lower price than that listed in your catalog, but you may, for example, be able to offer very fast delivery when needed.

If you know that you may have pricing problems, such as competition that offers lower prices, be sure to be prepared to answer the challenge of such problems. Find creative and justifiable reasons why your product or service is worth more, and explain these to your prospect. Perhaps your product is of better quality, will last longer, includes features not offered by the competition, and so on. Perhaps your product or service is the market leader, and the buyer is paying for the assurance of the seller's reliability and responsibility.

Practice in your mind possible dialogues related to pricing problems. If you are able to handle these creatively with good answers, you will be able to close your sales.

KEEP ATTENTION ON *YOUR* SALE, NOT YOUR COMPETITOR'S

Many salespeople fall into the trap of selling, and holding the prospect's attention, by disparaging the competition. They talk about how poor the competitive product is, how poor the supplier's service has been, and how questionable the delivery date promised is. Don't make the mistake of using this type of selling!

Not only will you likely be distorting the truth if you use negative selling, but you will also be focusing attention on your competitor. Sure, you are saying bad things about the competition. But the prospect may not remember whether you said bad or good things, just that the competitor's name was mentioned and is now familiar.

For example, a purchasing agent for a large firm agreed to see a sales representative, who then made a very negative presentation. For 45 minutes, the rep talked about the weaknesses of the competitor.

Finally, the buyer said, "Joe, I've heard about your competition for nearly an hour. They really have you worried, don't they? Now, have you got anything to tell me about your products and why I should be interested in them? Or do you just want to talk about the competition today?"

Getting Attention with Advice

A positive approach to holding the prospect's attention is to offer your continuing services as a consultant. This approach is often very effective as you close a sale and is even more effective once you have become established as a reliable source of advice.

"I'll be glad to check the English on your advertisements," one of my advertising space salesmen told an East European prospect. "Your English is excellent, but sometimes advertising copy translations can create a problem. Just send along any copy you'd like me to see, and I'll make suggestions that you can incorporate."

When this offer was made, the sale had not yet been closed, but the rep's assumption that the prospect was ready to buy closed the sale. Such an offer cannot be made with arrogance but must be made with a genuine interest in the client as well as with humility.

Any salesperson can offer to periodically check shipment records so that the buyer does not have to keep exact records of when to reorder consumable products, for example. If knowledgeable about the industry, salespeople can offer advice about marketing, the best marketplaces, and even product use, just because they have seen how the product is used by other companies. Of course, it is important not to give away proprietary information in such a case.

Offering free advice to buyers is useful in many ways. If you can anticipate the clients' problems and fears, and help them, they will feel at ease with you. When prospects feel that they have your support, they will be more secure about making decisions to buy from you.

SHOW AND TELL TO HOLD ATTENTION

No matter how much you discuss your product, nothing will replace showing the actual product to hold the prospect's attention. If the product is too intangible or too large to carry to the client, and the prospect cannot come to your home operation, a picture or literature must be substituted. Audiovisual presentations can also be used, although these are often too awkward and bulky to carry.

Whether you show your products or rely on literature, be sure to prepare a set of "leave-behinds," such as information sheets, models of the product, and other types of sales literature. Use the leave-behind package in selling and closing. Get prospects involved in the act by asking them questions as you show the literature.

Another effective way to use leave-behinds is to make notes on the sheets, including prices or comparisons with competitive products. These handwritten notes will interest the prospect and are likely to draw his or her attention to the literature after you leave as well as during the call.

A good paper-and-pencil method of holding attention involves drawing up a "balance sheet." Using a piece of paper from the prospect's desk, or one of the leave-behinds, draw up a simple plus-and-minus ledger (see Figure 4) showing the reasons for

Figure 4. A simple plus-and-minus ledger prepared in front of the prospect helps you close the sale and also serves as an effective leave-behind.

```
Reasons to Buy
  XYZ - Typewriter

      −          |          +
                 |
                 | 1. Interchangeable
                 |    type elements.
                 |
                 | 2. Self-correction
                 |    features.
                 |
                 | 3. 10% discount if
                 |    purchased by 6/1.
                 |
                 | 4. Service contract
                 |    at no cost.
```

buying your product or service. This can be left for the buyer to study later, either to reaffirm the wise decision to buy or to help persuade if the sale has not been closed.

If the prospect asks questions, answer when you can. If you don't know the answer, readily admit this and ask if you can use the phone to call your office for the proper information. (Naturally, if this is not a local call, mention that you will call collect or will use your telephone credit card.) This immediate action indicates that you and your company take care of questions and problems without delay.

Once your products and literature have been "shown" and your answers have been "told," the scene should be set to close the sale. If you hesitate too long, you will lose momentum and also the sale.

3

Using product options to close

There is more to closing than listening or getting the prospect's attention. It is also necessary to learn where your buyer's interests actually lie. Does your product or service fit the needs of the client? Can your product be easily modified to accommodate his or her requirements?

In most cases, I have learned from experience, you must select from your product line or even make some product or service modifications in order to meet the prospect's exact needs and thus more easily close the sale.

How does such product modification or the use of product options help you close? Let's assume that your prospect is a truck manufacturer and that you are trying to sell him tires to be used on his line of trucks. The prospect, however, tells you that the specifications on one of the tires you are trying to sell do not meet those required for use on the truck. The reasons for this statement could be many. The prospect may be convinced that a specific type of tire or tire design is best for the work for which the truck will be used, or he may believe that the truck will be used in climatic conditions unsuitable for the type of tire you want to sell.

At this point, it is important that you get the prospect to tell you what specific qualities he needs. Once you accomplish this, you can begin to sell the tire that most nearly meets those needs. This is an important step from a psychological standpoint, too,

Using Product Options to Close

since a prospect will begin thinking about purchasing from you once he or she begins telling you about specific product needs. After the prospect has expressed a need, it is up to you to fill it and close the sale. In the case of selling tires, you might describe the advantages of the tread of a specific tire in your line. This may be a new and better tread design that the prospect has not seen. Or you may find that the buyer wants a heavier tire than you had anticipated and be able to offer a similar product from your firm's line.

As you describe the options to the prospect, you should mentally visualize the contract and believe, in your own mind, that you have made the sale. Tell yourself that it is just a matter of putting together all the pieces and providing the client with the product options that he or she wants. At this point, there is no time for hesitation or doubt. You must move ahead.

Ask your client how he or she really pictures the delivered product. Keep stressing that you realize your client wants your product's basic design but can understand the desire to add optional features to best suit production needs. Sell the values of your product, but leave room for the prospect's own desires.

In addition to product options, be sure to offer your prospect advantages. Make a list, either mentally or on paper, of all the benefits the prospect will receive when he or she buys your product or service. Offer these benefits as if they were product options. In other words, sell satisfaction, and don't be shy about the advantages of your product. Talk about these advantages with enthusiasm. Let the buyer know your product is a wonderful one.

It is often useful to get the prospect to tell you about a similar product he or she now owns. If you are selling copying machines, for instance, ask questions about the copier now in use. Ask about product features, performance, and service. If you listen carefully, the buyer will tell you all the old copier's good points, options you should assume that he or she will want on the new machine. The buyer will also tell you about poor features of the machine, options that should be corrected by the product features you offer the prospect.

LET THE PROSPECT CHOOSE THE OPTIONS

Many times prospects will choose product options that you know are not best for their intended uses. For example, you may be selling engines, and the prospect may want to use an engine that is too large or too small or not efficient in some other way for the truck he or she is manufacturing.

This is the time to remember that the customer is always right. You can suggest the engine you believe to be the best choice, and quickly tell why. With some prospects, this will eventually win you more business.

As a rule, however, you should listen to the prospect and try to provide him or her with the product options specified. Discuss costs and advantages of both the options the prospect wants and the alternative product options. But if the prospect's reasons make sense to him or her, and if the product options specified are available, don't argue. The prospect wants to purchase what he or she believes is needed and will not like the thought that you have tried to sell something different, unless a very clear advantage exists and you can prove this. In other words, let clients buy what they want.

Simple? Psychology in action? Yes, but these simple aspects of selling are what help to close the sale. If you do not agree to the prospect's terms at the right minute, the sale will surely be lost.

Another example of letting the prospect choose product options is when selling an intangible, such as an insurance policy. The company may be offering extra commissions for a specific type of policy—life insurance, automobile insurance, business insurance, or some other policy—but you cannot hope to make a sale if you try to sell a type of insurance the prospect doesn't need or want. Instead, listen to the buyer's needs, and let him or her choose the product options. Even within a specified insurance area, there are many choices the buyer can make.

Suppose that you are selling business insurance to a client. You may be able to offer liability, property damage, theft, fire, loss of inventory, partnership life, and even shrinking-market insurance. You will be very foolish indeed if you try to sell the prospect all of these at once.

Instead, do your homework. Before making the call, know something about the prospect. Study the business, the building, the location, and anything else you can put into a file to help you close the sale. Learn about competitive businesses if possible and about what sort of insurance they carry. All this information will let you talk intelligently with your prospect; you can begin by saying that you have a fairly good idea of the kind of business involved. Don't talk about details that are too explicit at this point; discuss basic facts so that your prospect knows you are concerned enough to have learned a bit about the industry.

Be very careful not to discuss anything you know about competitive businesses, or your prospect might think you will talk about business matters you learn from him or her. Also, do not initially discuss your product directly. Open with a general discussion and offer to give advice about your business as it relates to the prospect's needs. You can take notes, and listen carefully, as he or she tells you about those needs—the product options. In many cases, it is important to remind the prospect that this is only a "get acquainted" call and that you do not intend to do any business. This will allay any fears the prospect may have, while you obtain your information.

Before you leave, find out which of your products the prospect does not already own and which he or she needs or wants.

Turning Product Option Choices into Sales

Once the prospect tells you his or her needs, you can turn product options into a selling tool by suggesting: "Why not, at no permanent obligation to you, let me institute temporary insurance protection against liability, fire, and theft. I would like to do a study of your needs, and this might take seven to ten days. In the meantime, you will have basic coverage in case of some sudden emergency—all at a very minimal cost." Then state the cost; since it will be only ten days worth of insurance, the cost should be very low.

If presented smoothly, this method should allow you to turn the prospect's product option preferences into temporary coverage, and then into a permanent policy. Using this type of closing, you can make a sale without the prospect thinking you have pressured him or her.

Help Buyers Identify with Your Product

It is important that the buyer be able to identify with your product. As you discuss the various product options, be sure to personalize your presentation with anecdotes that relate to the buyer.

A shoe salesman determined that a new customer was also a salesperson and that she spent most of the day on her feet. "I've had good customers tell me that this style of shoe stays comfortable no matter how long you are on your feet," he commented about one of the pairs of shoes she was considering. "If you walk clear around the shop, you'll be able to notice that the design has no awkward spots that rub. Be sure to walk on the bare floor. Go over to that far aisle."

The prospect made the trip. "Have you tried these new patented cushioned-soled models before?" the salesman asked.

By this point of the presentation, the buyer knew the salesman understood her problems. She felt involved with the product and its features. The salesman was selling not only product options but customer satisfaction and a continuing buying relationship.

Follow-through is Important, Too

Follow-through is important when you use product options to sell. Stay in touch with your client once the sale has been completed so that the client understands that his or her interests are important to you. Don't overdo this with daily phone calls or by interrupting business schedules, of course. Rather, call once a few days after the sale is closed. Talk to the prospect if he or she is not busy, or leave word that this is a follow-up and you will return the call. Don't try to sell more during such a call. A follow-up call is merely an opportunity to show your interest and to establish good friendly feelings. Overselling will hurt you more than help you.

On your next visit to the buyer, be prepared with an analysis of how your product or service can help the buyer. Be ready to discuss basic requirements and the product options the client has chosen. Be ready to talk about ways to obtain these options at the best price. If it is applicable, use the word *investment* rather than *cost* or *price*.

Point out the advantages the product has with the options the client has chosen. Try to create a picture of such advantages, using words, charts, illustrations, and so on to strengthen the buyer's interests in your product.

Next, tell the prospect about your study of his or her needs. Throughout your presentation of the study, stop frequently to ask if the prospect agrees with you. Find out whether you are on the right track or whether you must change the presentation as you go to suit the prospect's needs and wishes. If you do not make these checks, you could be talking yourself out of a sale.

Let your prospect know that you are suggesting these customized options because you have his or her particular needs in mind and want to do your best to meet them. Be discreet and humble when telling this to your client. Buyers like to do business with people who care about their needs and who are not too aggressive or pushy.

The Sale Never Ends

Follow-through goes beyond the initial two or three calls. For a good salesperson, the sale never ends. Keep a file of your customers; records are important if you want to continue to sell to these customers. Begin with the facts of the sale and add records of the client's birthday, the birthdays of family members, and so on. Such records give you reasons to send cards or to telephone. By staying in touch, you will find out when the client's needs change and when some new product options can be sold.

Product Modification to Provide New Options

In some cases, no product options are available that meet a specific prospect's needs. It is, however, often possible to modify the product to provide such options.

As an example, let's look at how I modify Judith Sans Internationale skin-care franchises, when necessary. Franchisees come in all shapes and sizes and from varied backgrounds. Usually, their backgrounds are not in the skin-care industry. Their financing in most instances is very limited. Thus, the prospective franchisee often cannot afford to open the type of franchise operation that would be best in a specific geographical territory. When this is the case, it becomes necessary to modify the product without hurting the franchise concept and the reputation of the franchising firm.

A Judith Sans Internationale franchise costs about $55,000 (in mid-1980) for the franchise rights, products, and equipment. It is advisable for the franchisee to have another $25,000 for leasehold expenditures and three to six months' operating costs.

In some cases, the prospect is sold on the franchise but cannot afford the total package. There are many possible modifications, however, that will allow the prospect to buy the package on a smaller scale. For instance, it may be possible to rent a smaller salon space to begin operations or for the franchisee to offer fewer facilities for servicing clients. It may be possible for the franchisee to begin operations with less equipment and fewer products and personnel than might be considered ideal. Possibly he or she can acquire a smaller territory (with a lower franchise fee) to begin.

Automobile selling provides another example of product option and modification selling. The salesperson starts, of course, with a basic car that comes off the assembly line. From that point, it becomes a matter of working with the buyers to choose options that they want and can afford.

The use of product options and modifications is limited only by your imagination and how many changes you or your company can actually make in your product or service. And when the prospects choose options, they choose your products. This means that you haven't sold anything; rather, they have made purchases, and you have closed sales.

4

Price negotiations

Pricing and discounting are often essential elements of closing a sale, and it is important to understand the basic ways in which they can be used.

Should your firm discount? Pricing a product, using normal accounting procedures to cover expenses and allow for a profit, does not usually leave room for a discount. If you are selling products or services to business buyers, they will usually understand this principle, because it also applies to them. If you are selling to nonbusiness buyers, you may be required to explain that in order to be fair your pricing is geared to a nondiscount way of business. You may need to remind the prospect that if you are to discount, the initial price must be set very high, so that you can appear to reduce it. This is unfair, because one buyer may receive a greater "discount" than the next.

If your company does decide to discount, you will find that in a short time the firm will have a reputation for this type of selling. It is almost impossible to lose such a reputation once earned. It is even difficult for an individual salesperson to lose such a reputation, even if he or she changes jobs and begins selling for a firm that doesn't discount.

Discounts That Can Be Used in Selling

There are discounts that can be used to close a sale and that are fair to all buyers. These are the discounts I prefer my own salespeople to use when selling, and you may want to consider them if you have a voice in deciding whether or not to discount.

One of the most common discounts is for prompt payment of an invoice. During our inflationary times, this becomes even more important to your firm since outstanding invoices cost the going rate of interest, yet seldom bring any return no matter how late they are paid. Thus, if the annual interest rate is 18 percent or 1.5 percent per month, an invoice that is not paid for 30 days costs your company that 1.5 percent. If it is not paid for 90 days, it costs your firm 4.5 percent. Most companies can calculate the maximum allowable discount by averaging the amount of time most of their customers take to pay their bills. This figure has been climbing, and while it was once 60 days, many companies find the average payment time is often nearer 90 days now. If this is so, the firm can build the interest rate into the initial price and offer up to a 4.5 percent discount on invoices paid immediately. Or the company might offer a 3 percent discount if the invoice is paid within 10 days and actually come out ahead.

It is important for you to determine what your company's policy is on this type of discount and then to use it to your advantage when selling. If the company does not have a policy of this type, suggest it to your manager along with the figures to back up what you say.

How do you use such a discount to close a sale? As your prospect becomes more interested in the product or service you have to sell, watch for the point when the price seems to be the only barrier to your completing the sale. Then you can say, "This price can be reduced by 3 or 4 percent for a total savings of $120. By paying the invoice within a few days, that $120 will be in your pocket, and you will have the product you want."

BEATING THE PRICE BALK

In addition to discounting, there are many aspects of product or service pricing that you can use to help close a sale. Most often, you need methods to overcome price resistance, since this is usually the final blockade that prevents wrapping up a sale.

Buyers often remind a salesperson about the high cost of a specific product or order that is under consideration. This does not necessarily mean that the prospect is hinting at or expecting a discount, although many salespeople erroneously make this assumption. Rather, the prospect may simply be expressing a concern about the large outflow of money.

There are a number of ways to handle the situation when a buyer hesitates because of price. One of the most effective methods is to remind the buyer how advantageous the product or service will be. If the product will help the buyer increase his or her own profits, be sure to mention this as soon as the total purchase price becomes part of the conversation. If the product or service is for personal use, remind the buyer that the product is of good quality and therefore perhaps a bit more expensive. However, the quality means that over a period of time the cost will actually be less, since replacements will not be needed for some time.

Many prospects are frightened by large total sums, and it often helps to present your product or service on an item-by-item basis. For example, if a schedule of advertising costs $10,000, my sales staff refers to the cost on a per-advertisement basis, cutting the per-page price mentioned to perhaps $900.

If an insurance policy costs a few hundred dollars per year, you can refer to the monthly payments available when you are explaining costs to the buying family. As you refer to these lower payments, however, remember at the same time to mention frequently the benefits of the large total payout in the event of a fire, theft, death, and so on. In selling automobiles, furniture, or other products that can be purchased on credit, it is also wise to refer to monthly payment or budget amounts rather than the total purchase price.

At one point during my career I helped a salesman sell to me

Price Negotiations

by showing him how to use monthly payment selling. I wanted very much to buy a specific house, but my wife was against the purchase because the total cost seemed too high. In order to make the purchase, I had to sell the idea to my wife.

I asked the real estate agent how much the monthly payments would be. He worked out the figure. Next, I asked my wife (who was in charge of our housing budget) whether we could afford the amount of the monthly payment, reminding her that my income was increasing year by year. She said that of course we could afford that amount.

My retort was, "Well, what are we waiting for? Let's enjoy what we both feel is our dream home." And we did.

The salesman almost lost this sale because he didn't discuss pricing properly. He should have been listening to my wife's objections and have suggested the monthly payments himself. Fortunately for him, I helped him close the sale.

As a salesperson, you will seldom be lucky enough to have a buyer who helps you close. When selling any product or service, listen carefully for the prospect to mention the word *budget* or *cost*. This is most often a prospect's attempt to put off making the purchasing decision or to see if you will lower the price. The word *budget* or *cost* should trigger an alarm in your mind that tells you to go one step further to get the prospect's signature on the order. It should signal you to begin price negotiations.

Price Negotiations That Don't Cost You Money

Price bargaining usually means that the buyer wants the seller to reduce the price. But not all price negotiations cost money. For example, once your prospect begins to talk about his or her budget, you may be able to offer a service that your firm normally provides free but that the prospect would have to buy otherwise. Your firm may offer free marketing aids, such as surveys that provide information your prospect might have to buy elsewhere. Your company may offer inventorying services, holding and shipping goods as the buyer requires them, thereby eliminating the need for the buyer to rent or own excess warehouse space.

If your firm does offer such services, it is a good selling tool to compute the cost of the service and then explain that you are saving the buyer this amount. The wise salesperson will not mention services until price negotiations begin and the situation calls for an additional selling tool. In computing the cost of warehousing, include the cost not only of space rental or ownership but also of the labor that is needed to move the merchandise.

Another word of caution is in order. If your firm offers a number of services, don't mention them all at one time. If you do, the prospect may decide that your company has excessively high profits.

Price negotiations may involve more than the basic product or service price. Recently, I read about the president of an airplane manufacturing company. He knew that his firm was about to close a sale with a large airline on a number of the company's planes, but the airline was holding back because of cost. By checking the fuel usage of the planes already being flown by the airline and comparing them with the figures on his own firm's planes, the president was able to offer a written pledge of 35 percent fuel savings with the new planes and promise that if this savings was not made his firm would pay the difference. Naturally, this promise was the price negotiation step that closed the sale.

Give-to-get selling is one of my own favorite price negotiation techniques. I used this method in selling to government officials of the People's Republic of China. I wanted to publish Chinese-language mining and construction magazines, which would be distributed in China. I had to sell these officials on giving permission for distribution within China and on providing names and addresses of those buying influences within the country who should receive the magazines. In order to persuade them, I gave something in return. I offered them free technical information (in the magazines) useful to people in responsible positions. I also offered to do the translating, typesetting, and printing (which had to be done somewhere anyway) in China, giving them a source of hard currency. Additionally, we would be spending hard currency for the distribution of the magazines. I "gave" them business I had to buy from some source.

When using give-to-get selling, it is important to know your cost and profit needs so that you can negotiate only what you can really afford to give. Usually, it is best to be open and honest with your prospects and to tell them that you can afford to give a certain amount, whether this is in the form of services, contract deals, or other items. If your judgment tells you that your prospects are sincere, this is the best approach. Sincere buyers will appreciate both your need to make a profit and also what you can give them in return for the order.

When negotiating, whether using give-to-get or other techniques, it is important, as in any aspect of selling, to listen. Listen for key words that signal the possible close of the sale. In the case of my offer to the Chinese officials, there came a point when the translator said that the head official found my ideas interesting and that they wanted to have a meeting by themselves to discuss further a plan that would allow some final action. This was what I had been waiting for. Once I heard those words, I knew the possibility of closing the sale was near. My reply was that I would like a recess, too, since it would give me an opportunity to work out a schedule for an orderly translation of our editorial material into Chinese and for the printing and distribution.

Once this recess had been completed, negotiations were simple. I knew that my prospects wanted to buy, and I closed the sale.

PRICE NEGOTIATIONS WITH A GROUP

Selling to a group can be a very different matter than selling to an individual, and price negotiation techniques must be varied to suit this situation. Recently, I sold a franchise to a group of six people, three husbands and three wives, who had joined together to buy a Judith Sans Internationale skin-care franchise operation.

The advertisement that these prospects answered stated that franchises are available for a minimum of $50,000. Even though the word *minimum* is used on purpose, many prospects answer such an ad believing that they can buy a franchise with only a percentage of that money as a down payment. In this case, financing for the full package was not available within the group, and it was necessary to use price negotiation to close the sale.

This could have been done in two ways. One way would have been to offer the group a smaller package than the one advertised. The second way, and the way I chose, was to negotiate elements of the price. Many possibilities were open to me here. First, we could decide to delay payment on part of the franchise fee, thus partially financing the operation from the home office. Another possibility was to help the buyers lease equipment, to eliminate some of the initial capital investment costs.

As I made these suggestions, two members of the group were hesitant, while the others seemed to agree with what I was offering. To close the sale, I knew that all six members of the group would have to be persuaded. I accomplished this by watching the group members and listening to their conversations. Next, I chose the person who seemed most convinced and who seemed to have the best sales personality himself. I began asking him questions aimed at eliciting answers that would restate my position. His answers helped me convince the rest of the group members that they should accept either partial financing from the home office or help with leasing their equipment.

Price Negotiations

This example shows once again how essential it is to listen to your prospects and to adapt what they say in a way that will help you show them the advantages of buying from you.

NEGOTIATING WITHOUT AN ESTABLISHED PRICE STRUCTURE

At times, price negotiations are necessary even though no price has been established for the product or service. This type of selling could be used for a new or experimental product or for investment items, such as art, antique jewelry, coins, and stamps.

Recently, I purchased a dozen or so Rembrandt lithographs for a very low price from a Parisian who was badly in need of cash. On my return to the United States, I chose a few to frame and keep in my home and decided to sell the remainder. I knew that I had bought them for quite a low price, but I did not know what they were worth in the marketplace.

I decided to sell them by advertising to people interested in art. The first person who approached me looked at the lithographs and quickly offered me a price. Even though this price would have more than paid for the group I had bought, I believed this man was a dealer and had some idea of their value. I didn't sell any to him, but I had his offer as a starting point to establish a price.

When the next person contacted me, I quadrupled the price offered to me by the first prospect. Naturally, I expected a counteroffer—which I got. We began our dealing. I kept mentioning the name Rembrandt and the investment potential of these lithographs. I also established, by listening, that the prospect enjoyed "gambling" with stocks and bonds as investments.

At the right moment, I reminded this prospect that I had been offered a fairly decent price by an art dealer. I then suggested that the prospect's purchase would be something of a gamble and something of an investment. This hit his love of playing his instincts, and he was ready to take the chance. I closed the sale at a price much higher than that offered by the dealer—because I negotiated the price rather than accepting the first reasonable offer.

5

Giving something for nothing

The title of this chapter is intriguing—even to me. All of us should know that there is no such thing as "something for nothing." Yet it is possible to give the buyer, after he or she has purchased a product or service, something for nothing. I also call this give-to-get selling.

I have described some aspects of give-to-get selling in earlier chapters, but this technique is so successful in helping the salesperson close sales that it deserves a much more extensive treatment.

Forcing a Final Decision

Giving services can help force a final decision. A good example is what often happens in an automobile showroom. The buyer has probably already been sold on a specific car by radio, television, or print media advertising. The salesperson, however, must settle the question of the price and the extras—in other words, he or she must close the sale.

In many cases, a salesperson will use all the correct tactics of listening and asking questions that result in positive answers, but the prospect may still not be willing to say yes. What can be done?

This is the time for the salesperson to pull some goodies out of the bag. He or she can begin by telling the prospective buyer about the service advantages offered by the dealership. It often helps when the salesperson escorts the buyer into the service department to show how efficiently it is run and even introduces the prospect to the head of the department. Offering these continued services, which are hopefully better than those of the competition, can be considered giving something for nothing.

The automobile salesperson may also be able to offer to have the car owner driven to his or her place of work or home whenever the car is being serviced. This cost will, of course, be absorbed into the general operating costs, but the customer will feel that he or she has gotten something extra. Personal services of this sort are the easiest to offer as an extra, both because so few firms give good personal service today and because such service can be performed without too much extra effort or cost.

For another example of give-to-get techniques, let's look at selling advertising space. The salesperson begins with the usual selling routine. He or she tells the prospect why the magazines are right for specific products and why readers (their buyers) read the magazine and thus their advertisements. Using good selling techniques, the salesperson will go through the magazine with prospects, asking which articles they like best and why. As the prospects answer, they are selling themselves on positive points about the magazine, and that helps to close the sale.

As a final convincing point, the salesperson can offer to position the advertiser's ad in a prime location in the magazine—opposite the opening page of the feature editorial, for example—at no extra cost. This truly gives the advertiser something for nothing, yet it does not cost the salesperson or his or her company even one cent.

Marketing services can also help you sell. Frequently, the salespeople on my staff offer to do a free "did-you-buy" study for their advertising clients. In this case, our company sends a follow-up letter to readers who asked for more information about a product that was advertised (see Figure 5). The letter asks if

Giving Something for Nothing

Would you take a minute to give us information we can use to improve delivery of product information? You may remember that some time ago you filled in a postcard requesting information about a product you saw advertised in WORLD CONSTRUCTION. Your answers to a few questions may help us to get product information to you promptly when you need it.

1. Did you receive the information you wanted from FMC LINK-BELT?

    ( ) Yes   ( ) No

2. Did you know the FMC LINK-BELT dealer in your area?

    ( ) Yes   ( ) No

3. Did an FMC LINK-BELT distributor or dealer contact you?

    ( ) Yes   ( ) No

4. If Yes, how were you contacted?
    ( ) By Salesperson   ( ) By Telephone   ( ) By Mail
    ( ) Not Contacted   ( ) Other_____

5. As a result, did you purchase an FMC LINK-BELT product?

    ( ) Yes   ( ) No

6. If you were not contacted are you still interested in FMC LINK-BELT products?

    ( ) Yes   ( ) No

7. Did you purchase similar products from some other company?

    ( ) Yes   ( ) No

8. Is it possible that you will still purchase this type of equipment from FMC LINK-BELT in the future?

    ( ) Yes   ( ) No

Name_____ Title_____

Company or organization_____

Location_____

THANK YOU FOR YOUR HELP. YOUR ANSWERS WILL HELP US TO IMPROVE DELIVERY OF PRODUCT INFORMATION TO PEOPLE WHO NEED IT.

Figure 5. Questionnaire used as a nonstop selling technique.

the reader received the literature requested and if he or she bought the product advertised or a similar product from a competitor.

Marketing services make good giveaways for many types of businesses. For example, American Express offers many marketing services to stores, hotels, and restaurants that honor American Express cards. These services include free mentions in American Express ads and market surveys and studies compiled from buying records of card users.

Adapting Give-to-Get Selling Techniques

You can adapt such giveaway ideas to your own product or service. For example, if you sell real estate and the home you are selling is not a new one, your firm might offer to send in a team of cleaning people to be sure that everything is in good condition before the new buyer moves. No matter how clean the former owners were, a mess will be left from the process of moving out. For the cost of $100 or perhaps even less, you can offer something so appealing that it can easily help you close the sale on a $50,000 or much larger purchase, with its 10 percent commission. And unless new contractors in your area are more careful about cleanup than most contractors, this same service can also help sell new properties.

In addition, it is possible to offer some other services to the buyers of new homes. For example, the salesperson can offer to make arrangements to have utilities connected. These are small items that may take only a bit of the salesperson's time, but they will mean a great deal to the prospective buyer and may make the difference between your getting the sale and the purchaser giving his or her business to someone else.

In adapting give-to-get ideas for your own product, remember to stress personal service giveaways, which are becoming increasingly rare. Make a list of the types of giveaways that you might offer for your product, and keep this list where you can read it regularly. You can easily put together such a list just by thinking about what kind of giveaways you would like if you were the buyer.

What this really means is that you humanize your selling. It helps to remind prospects that you are not only a salesperson but a person concerned about pleasing your customers—because of your reputation, because of the reputation of your company, and because it is good business to make your customers happy.

Don't Let Giveaways Ruin a Sale

Even with all the assistance that giving something for nothing can provide, giveaways can ruin the chance to close a sale if they are not handled correctly. The secret is to remember that the customer is important and not get too involved in sticking to arbitrary rules surrounding what can be given away.

A simple example will explain how giving something for nothing can ruin a good sale. In this case, I was the buyer rather than the seller.

I had been making calls with a salesperson on my staff, and we had been driving through the Midwest. As we drove, we saw signs advertising vegetables, including new sweet corn, which was in season. The signs served their intended purpose—by the end of the day, we were both hungry for sweet corn. We decided that we would be sure to order it with our dinner that evening. And this was in our minds as we entered a well-known restaurant.

It was Friday evening, and we had no clients to take to dinner, so we felt we could spoil ourselves with a good meal as a reward for a week of very hard work. We looked at the menu and began to plan our order—a large steak, a bottle of wine, and most importantly a fresh ear of corn. The price of this dinner, including the wine, was about $25 per person. As we looked at the menu, we noticed another item: "Special: Barbequed chicken and spareribs, and sweet corn—all you can eat—only $3.95."

Reading the special, I thought that it made a good loss leader to attract new customers or to thank old patrons for their support. (I was later told that this was a traditional special, run once a year when the first corn was ready.) But my salesman and I had decided on steak. We gave the waitress our orders, specifying that we would also like an ear of corn.

"Oh no," the waitress said. "The corn is only available with the special."

We replied that we wanted the steak and that we were, of course, willing to pay whatever the restaurant wanted to charge for the corn. The waitress said she would check.

After a trip to the kitchen, she returned and informed us that we could only have corn with the special.

After much discussion, we asked to see the manager. We repeated our request to him.

He looked at us and with a very straight face said that the waitress was right—the only way we could get corn was by ordering the special. No matter what we offered to pay for the corn, he could not deviate from the rules. Telling him how much we wanted corn made no difference.

By this time, it was late. We decided to stay, forgo the steaks and wine and have the special. We wanted sweet corn. The special was great; the corn was wonderful. We ate and ate. Our total bill was under $10 rather than $50 or more.

Had the owner observed this transaction, he or she would probably have been most unhappy. By giving something for nothing, the restaurant had lost the biggest part of a prospective sale.

You can avoid this same type of error by using give-to-get selling wisely but having enough sense not to stick to arbitrary rules or giveaway gimmicks when they may hurt your chances of closing the sale.

6

Nonstop selling

Most salespeople stop too soon and thus do not close as many sales as they could. Studies show that the average sale is made on the fifth call. Do you make that many calls on each of your prospects? Sometimes? Always? Never?

If you want to close more often, you must practice nonstop selling and continue to make calls, renegotiating until you get a yes answer.

Be repetitive. Prospects will not remember everything you have said, even though it may seem so to you since you make basically the same sales presentation as many as four or five times per day. Don't be afraid to tell your prospective buyers—again and again, if necessary—the main reasons they will benefit from purchasing from you. You can repeat your main selling points profitably by using examples, anecdotes, and so on.

Use emotional appeals as you repeat the good points of your product or service. In order to sell well, you must convey to your prospect a strong positive feeling about your product. Before I make a sales call, I often jot down a list of emotional appeals that I believe might influence the prospect.

Expect to close the sale each time you make a call, but don't write a prospect off if he or she doesn't buy on your first call, or your third.

The nonstop selling method can take quite a long time. There are ways, however, you can speed it up without making personal calls. For example, you can use sales letters, promotional mailings, and telephone calls to supplement personal visits. Sales letters are an art in themselves as a less expensive way of "calling" on clients between personal calls. (Appendix A provides some of my own most effective letters that help close sales, as well as the best of the letters used by my staff over the years.)

Dealing with Objections

One of the main problems you will face in nonstop selling is dealing with the prospect's objections. You know the type of prospects I mean—they always find something wrong with your product or service, something that prevents them from purchasing it, for now, at least. Or they have budgetary reasons that keep them from buying.

A key element in successfully dealing with objections is a method we have already discussed—listening. But once you've heard the prospect's objection, the next step is to do something creative about it.

For example, assume the prospect tells you he or she can't buy because of a limited budget. That is some information you can use. You have something to work with. This must be the beginning point of your sale and of your marathon selling campaign.

Build on what the prospect has told you. Tell him or her that you understand the situation. Then, let the prospect know that you feel you have not done your job properly, because, had you done it right, the prospect would already have purchased your product or service. Explain that had the prospect known all the reasons your product or service was best for the person with a limited budget, he or she would have bought from you rather than choosing other products or services. Next list those reasons. Since limited budgets are commonly cited as objections, any salesperson should have a prepared list of reasons his or her product is economical—for example, the product is of such good quality that it lasts a long time: its purchase price is lower than that of competitive products: free service is included, which makes its costs lower over a period of time.

This explanation will probably not allow you to close a sale during that call, but such efforts are apt to have long-term benefits. If you explain the cost advantages of your product now, the prospect will be more likely to buy from you when new budgets become available—if you remember to follow through with more calls. This means that it is essential for you to ask the buyer when his or her budgetary year ends and to make a personal call prior to that time. It is also wise to help the prospect remember you during the interim by sending occasional letters, promotional material, and so on.

PUT YOURSELF IN THE PROSPECT'S PLACE

Recently, I was in Italy on business. While eating lunch in a tiny trattoria, I began to talk with a man sitting near me, and I mentioned that I was the publisher of four magazines. This gentleman told me that he was a designer and manufacturer of specialty furniture, and he described the advertising space salesman who first persuaded him to advertise. This was a nonstop salesman indeed! And he was one who put himself in the buyer's place, assuming the buyer's needs as if they were his own.

The salesman first came in contact with this manufacturer, not because of his wish to sell, but because his wife wanted a piece of furniture that was different. He had heard about this designer, who at that time had a relatively small operation. He visited the designer and arranged for the furniture to be built.

After receiving the furniture, the salesman thought about the fact that many people want specialty furniture and that they should know about this designer. But he knew it would take forever to get the word around by personal recommendations. Because he was a salesman, this man visited the designer again and began to tell him about his publication and how it could provide a marketplace for specialty furniture.

The salesman's publication was the most costly in the industry. The designer, who had never done any advertising, was not about to part with the kind of money required. He said he was very content with his present small operation, making a nice profit, and had no need to gamble on the additional business that advertising might bring.

The salesman, not to be set aside by a simple no, started his nonstop selling campaign. He planned his strategy for each visit with the designer, listening and learning ways he might close the sale. On each visit he repeated the pitch about what advertising in his magazine could do for the designer's business.

"He acted as if he were me," the manufacturer told me. "He talked about my problems as if they were his problems."

After a year, and 14 calls, the designer agreed to place an advertisement in the salesman's publication. Perhaps the designer felt such empathy from the salesman that he placed advertising for that reason alone. Whatever his initial reason, the advertising delivered the promises made by the salesman. The manufacturer now owns seven factories and told me that he is much more successful than he had ever dreamed of being. He is convinced of the value of advertising, thanks to a nonstop salesman, and told me that he believes anything can be sold with the right advertising.

Sell Nonstop for Continuing Sales

Nonstop selling is important for continuing sales, too. Most of us depend on repeat business. But not all salespeople remember that even good customers occasionally need to be resold on the virtues of a product or service.

One salesman learned this the hard way when he breezed into

a customer's office saying, "What size order are you going to give me today, Fred?"

Fred had just discovered faulty products in his last shipment and was in no mood for the salesman's cocky, self-sure approach. Had the salesman entered the office saying "What can I do to help you today?" the next sale might still have been closed. But because he forgot to use a nonstop selling approach, the buyer firmly told him that he would be placing no order. A competitor got the business.

Nonstop selling becomes even more important when you are selling a product or service with a very large price tag; the buyer may be investing his or her life savings in a new home, a franchise, or any other large purchase. Such a buyer needs to be told many times about the advantages of what he or she will be purchasing. If you will put yourself in the buyer's situation, you will find it much easier to understand what is needed.

Keep Offering Assurance

As you plan your nonstop selling program, remember that the main thing your prospective buyer needs is assurance that the decision to buy from you is the right decision. Begin by telling the prospect that you will work to be sure that your product or service meets his or her needs in every way. To make your presentation more credible, describe how your product or service has helped other buyers. If necessary, offer to put the prospect in touch with satisfied buyers.

Tell your prospect that you want to be a partner as well as a salesperson—that is, by pleasing him or her, you hope to become partners in a continuing business relationship. If the product or service is something new for the prospect, reassure him or her about using it. Compliment the buyer about what he or she has already accomplished and describe how much more can be done with the use of your product or service. But whatever you choose to say, it's important to be sincere.

It's often said that a good con artist can sell anything once. But a good salesperson wants more than one sale. He or she wants the repeated business that comes from nonstop selling. If this continued business requires an investment of time, and it does, then you must be willing to make that investment.

Remember that prospects buy only from people in whom they have confidence, and keep selling yourself as a helpful, reliable person. This will help reassure prospects and repeat buyers alike as much as anything that you can do.

Don't Oversell

Often salespeople get too carried away with offering assurance and with other aspects of nonstop selling. When this happens, oversell is the result. A good example was described to me by the owner of an equipment manufacturing firm.

"This one salesman is just too much," he told me. "Even though he has the best product and good prices, I can't bring myself to buy from him. I think all he does is fly from airport to airport and make telephone calls. He called me from Atlanta on a Monday. 'This is Fred Stover. You know we were discussing the best new tire design for your trucks. I had a few minutes between planes here in Atlanta, so I thought I'd call you and see if you'd made a decision.'"

My associate was very amusing as he mimicked the salesman's eager tone of voice.

"I told him I hadn't had a chance to think about it and that he'd have to get back to me," the manufacturer continued. "On Wednesday, he called again. 'This is Fred Stover. I'm waiting for a plane here in Dallas, and I wondered if you'd decided which tire tread is right for you.'

"The next week he called me from New Orleans and Chicago with the same song and dance. I admire persistence, but that guy's a pest, and I won't buy from him at all."

Oversell is a frequent problem for some salespeople during

social events. At a recent trade show, we were entertaining a good customer. The salesman started a sales pitch during the meal, which was being served in an elegant French restaurant. I literally kicked him under the table to let him know that he was slipping over that fine line between nonstop selling and oversell. The event was a thank-you and business relationship consolidation dinner, and a sales presentation was definitely out of place.

It may take time to develop a sixth sense about the dividing line between aggressive nonstop selling and oversell. But such a sense is essential to success. It is necessary to take the lead and to keep reminding your prospect of the advantages of buying your product or service. It is also important to never feel sorry for a prospect who claims budgetary or other problems as an excuse for not buying. You must clear away the obstacles, turning negatives into positives. But you must learn to know when too much aggressiveness will cause the buyer to say, as my manufacturer friend did, "That guy's a pest, and I won't buy from him at all."

Internal Corporate Nonstop Selling

If you sell for a large corporation, you can put your skills to work selling internally to corporate management. By this, I don't mean selling yourself for such personal benefits as promotions or salary increases—this goes on within corporations, too, of course, and is called corporate politics—but using your selling abilities to help your company grow. When you have an idea that you believe will make profits for your company, sell it to top management. Sometimes the idea must be sold even above the top of the ladder, to the corporate board of directors. Such a selling process can take a long time because corporate decision makers do not always really know what will result in the greatest benefits for the company. An example from my own experience will show you how nonstop selling can be used in such a situation.

As publisher of a magazine that was rapidly rising to the number-one spot in the industry, I began to consider another publication in a related field. I believed we were ready to make the move.

Our corporate history was such that new publications were not favored. In about 40 years of business, the company had never started a new magazine. A selling plan was needed, and it had to have many facets. The first step was to sell the idea of owning and publishing a periodical in the chosen field. My staff made a study of the marketplace and other magazines presently covering it. On the basis of this study, we argued that another publication was needed because a specific segment of the industry—equipment—was not being properly covered by the magazines already being published.

A second study showed that readers of existing publications in the industry believed that a magazine on equipment was needed. Finally, a study of the number of advertisers within the industry showed that there was a large marketplace for us.

Since I knew corporate policy about starting publications, we began by selling the idea of buying a magazine to fill the need. Corporate management enthusiastically approved that idea, because of our nonstop selling, and we approached an existing publication with the idea of converting it into the type of magazine we wanted.

Eventually, more selling led to the O.K. to start our own magazine. We used the very techniques I have been describing to you for selling products and services, but the methods were used to sell a potentially profitable idea to our corporate management. Within two years of that first sale, the corporation started three additional new magazines.

You too can make internal sales that will help your company, using nonstop selling techniques to close.

Nonstop Selling Equals Greater Rewards

Nonstop selling takes longer than one-call sales, but the results are greater. Even though you may make many sales calls,

Figure 6. Begin by spending most of your time on short-term sales goals to build the financial base you need. Gradually devote more time to long-term goals that will result in a much greater volume of business.

TIME PLAN TO REACH SELLING GOALS

Weekly hours devoted to:

	Short-term goals (sales to be made within one month)	Intermediate-term goals (sales to be made within three months)	Long-term goals (sales to be made within one year)
Jan	25	10	5
Feb	25	10	5
Mar	20	10	10
Apr	20	10	10
May	18	10	12
June	18	10	12
July	16	12	12
Aug	16	12	12
Sept	14	12	14
Oct	14	12	14
Nov	12	12	16
Dec	12	12	16

the repeated business that usually results from such efforts will mean more business and money for both your company and yourself.

If you believe that you cannot afford to take a long time to close your sales, then consider this bit of advice. Set yourself the goal of working on at least one nonstop selling campaign a month, and devote the rest of your time to making fast, short-term sales. Figure 6 will show you how you can accomplish these multiple goals and pyramid your sales.

Too many of us cannot see the forest for the trees in selling. We should be as anxious to make quick sales as we are to make long-term ones, but we must remember that in the long pull, our incomes do not depend on those quickie sales. We depend most on nonstop selling, which means repeated sales.

7

Follow-up selling

Follow-up selling includes several aspects of selling—making sure a closed sale stays closed, account servicing, and repeat sales. Without careful attention to these important areas, you will spend far too much time on one-shot sales and will never sell the large volume possible with effective follow-up selling. Follow-up selling is closely related to nonstop selling, but these techniques are used most often with long-standing clients rather than with new accounts or prospects.

Selling Is Like a Love Affair

Good selling is like a love affair. Think back to how you acted when you first fell in love. You didn't say "that's nice" and walk away. You probably spent a great deal of time and effort trying to please the object of your affection. Follow-up selling techniques are comparable efforts in fanning the flames of your buyer's affection—and your bank account.

There are a number of specific follow-up techniques that you can use. But first, look at yourself and make sure you know the basic personal facts that will help you become the successful suitor in your selling love affair.

To begin, be a smiling person. Buyers, like most people, enjoy being with people who smile and are pleasant more than with those who frown and complain.

Next, sell yourself. You probably worked hard at persuading your first love that you were the best. Carry out the same kind of campaign with your prospects. Be sure to be sincere, though, so that clients will have confidence in you.

Be positive and expect to make sales. The most popular people in your school days were probably those who showed self-confidence. The same principle holds true in selling. Besides, self-confidence is contagious. In love, a self-confident attitude lets both parties feel good about each other. In sales, your self-confidence can help your buyer feel good about you and about him- or herself.

Practice saying *you* a lot. In a love affair, your mind or heart centers on your partner. You try to see things from his or her perspective. Buyers also like you to look at the situation from their point of view.

Motivate prospects using emotion as well as reason. In a love affair, your partner may respond to attention and interest. The same holds true when selling.

Remember that what motivates changes with the times. A soda at the corner drugstore may have turned on your first heartthrob, but it probably wouldn't today. Keep yourself, your ideas, and your selling techniques up to date.

Timing is crucial in a love affair—and in selling. Don't try to close a sale when a prospect is upset about something or preoccupied with urgent business not related to your sale. In other words, be as considerate with a buyer as you would be with a lover.

Be persistent. If you are personally very interested in a man or woman, you'll pursue them persistently. You must pursue the prospect as well.

Ask for the order—this is a selling rule that can never be repeated too often. Just as you'll never have a date if you don't ask for one, so will you never have a sale unless you ask for the order.

Follow-up Selling

Close on implied consent. You don't ask for signed permission to kiss your lover; you watch for signs of implied consent and go ahead. In selling, you must watch for signals that imply consent to buy. These include such statements as:

Do you have this in blue?
It's the same model my brother owns.
How much of a discount do I get on this special sale?
I like this suit best.
Is financing available?

The next step is to take action. Just as you can use the old line "Your place or mine?" to advance a love affair, the salesperson can wind up a sale with such lines as:

Do you want to take it with you to save the delivery fee?
Is this charge or cash?
Would you like it gift wrapped?

Build the relationship into a lasting one. When love is real, it grows. You can help your sales relationships grow, too, by making them as good as possible for the buyers as well as for yourself.

Follow-up Can Keep the Closed Sale Closed

If you're like most of us in selling, there have been times when you have left a prospect believing you had closed the sale. But somehow, after you were away from the buyer's office or home, the prospect changed his or her mind.

The change may have been due to carelessness on your part. A striking example of this was a sale "closed" by one of my staff.

Even though I had taught the salesman that his card and a copy of the magazine should be presented to the prospect on every call, he decided he'd called on the client several times and that a card was not necessary. My representative made a good verbal presentation, and the prospect agreed to place a schedule of advertising in our magazine. The salesman was thrilled and left the client's office with a big smile, confident that the necessary paperwork would be sent to our production department.

When no paperwork arrived to verify the salesman's verbal order, and the next issue of the magazine was ready to go to press, the salesman finally called the agency. To his dismay, he found he'd closed the sale—but for his competition.

Unfortunately, with no business card or magazine before him, the buyer had been mentally envisioning a competititive magazine as he listened to my salesman's verbal presentation, and a few days later, instructed his advertising agency to submit the order to our competitor's magazine.

Does this story sound unbelievable? It did to me when I first heard the details. But, sorry to say, it is true.

The sale could have been closed for our magazine if the salesman had followed through. If he had presented his card and a copy of the magazine, the buyer would not have confused us with the competition in the first place. If he had promptly followed up his visit with a letter or phone call to thank the buyer for his business, the order would have been corrected.

Follow-up selling is important for many reasons. Consider your own buying habits. Once you've made a purchase, especially an expensive one, do you ever wonder if you made the right decision? Most people do, and proper follow-up can help assure them that their choices were correct. A simple phone call or letter to say "Thanks for the business. I know you'll be happy with your purchase. Let me know if I can be of help in any way" will not only reassure the buyer but also help you keep your closed sale closed and obtain repeat business.

Letters are often the most satisfactory way of immediately following up a closed sale. Appendix B provides the best follow-up sales letters developed by myself and my staff over the years.

Account Servicing as Follow-up Selling

Proper account servicing turns you into a consultant. Your first duty in account servicing is to make sure that each buyer receives his or her purchase as promptly as possible and in good condition. A telephone call is the first step, and it should be scheduled for two or three days after the delivery date. If the buyer has received the shipment, you will look good for making sure. If something has gone wrong with the shipment, you will be able to solve the buyer's problem before the buyer becomes angry and cancels the order.

When your product is one that is consumed or worn out, account servicing should also include follow-up when it is time to reorder. For instance, if a copying machine uses the manufacturer's brand of paper only, the salesperson should determine the average number of copies the client will make and build schedule into a tickler file so that he or she will contact the client in time to reorder paper. Such orders may be handled completely by telephone, eliminating a personal call but providing sales commissions and customer satisfaction.

Account servicing should also include customer problem solving or trouble shooting. Listen for hints about your client's problems. Then put your own creativity and industry knowledge to work to help your buyer solve those problems. Your suggestions should include whatever you believe will truly help the buyer solve the problems, not only suggestions that will lead to closing a sale. In other words, sell satisfaction with you and your service in addition to selling your product.

Whenever possible, visit your buyer and ask to see the product you've sold in action. If you've sold three new typewriters to an office, for example, ask the office manager (the buyer) to go with you to talk to the typists using the machines. Ask questions about how the machines are operating and explain any operating details they have missed in the instruction book. Such a look at the actual operations will not only put you in line for any new sales but also let you see for yourself what related equipment may be needed. You may note that the dictaphone units in use are outdated, and you may be able to suggest an office-wide system that will save the buyer money over the purchase of individual units but will mean additional closed sales.

Repeat Sales Go to Service-Oriented Salespeople

No matter how well you train yourself to ask for the business, you will not make repeat sales unless you provide the buyer with satisfaction as well as a product. As you continue to service your buyers' needs, their confidence in you will grow—another important element in repeat selling.

Don't forget to repeat your compliments when servicing a client. All buyers like to feel that they made the right decision by choosing your product. If you continually help buyers feel this way, your repeat sales will continue to climb.

II

The SALES MANAGER'S ROLE in CLOSING

Although I have addressed this section to the sales manager, you can benefit from reading the next three chapters whether you are a sales manager or a salesperson. For the sales manager, I've included the many techniques that have helped me train, motivate, and assist salespeople. These techniques were developed after many years of both selling and managing. They get to the heart of a sales manager's job and help him or her obtain top performance from the sales staff.

If you are a salesperson, it is absolutely vital that you read the chapters in this section. Even if your sales manager has given you good training, these chapters will help you absorb, as if you were working directly with me, all I've learned in a lifetime of selling and sales management.

8

Training salespeople to close

Training salespeople is not easy, but it can be very rewarding. Selling with your own methods is something every sales manager should already have learned. You may even have been able to train yourself to sell, because you know your own abilities and shortcomings.

SHOULD YOU BE A SALES MANAGER?

It is probably necessary to be a successful salesperson before you become a sales manager. But being a good salesperson will not automatically make you a good sales manager. A typical example is an insurance salesman I've known for many years. He was tops in his field and made the Million Dollar Round Table every year. Looking at his record, the home office decided to appoint him to a district manager's spot. With only three salespeople to supervise, my acquaintance was able to function in that position mainly by making joint calls with his salespeople and closing the sales for them. Looking only at his record of success, the home office promoted this man to a regional manager's job, with six districts of four salespeople each to supervise. Here, the progression halted. It was physically impossible for this man to make joint calls with 24 salespeople. He didn't know how to train or motivate his sales staff to successfully close sales on their own. Fortunately, my acquaintance realized that he was a salesman and not a sales manager and asked to be given a territory rather than a managerial job.

Another alternative would have been for my acquaintance to learn the basic steps of teaching salespeople to close. If you are learning these steps now, or if you hope to become a sales manager in the future, begin by practicing patience and fortitude—you will need both.

Measuring Sales Staff Trainability

Before you begin to train, you must be sure your sales staff is trainable. If you are in the very fortunate position of setting up a new sales staff, you can choose the most easily trained people by using guidelines set out in this chapter. If you have inherited a sales staff, take the time needed to analyze their performances and then promptly dismiss those you believe to be untrainable. While this may seem rather heartless, it is essential if you want to have a profitable operation.

The first step in checking sales staff trainability is to analyze your own thinking. What do you need in a salesperson? What qualifications, work attitudes, and skills, in your opinion, are most important? Make a list of these qualities in order of their importance to you. Figure 7 shows my own list. The qualifications I have listed are the elements that I have found to be necessary in a salesperson if he or she is to be both trainable and successful. In addition to the qualifications on the list, I assume that every sales manager insists that his or her salespeople have adequate intelligence, are able to converse easily with others, and have outgoing personalities. It is also essential to hire only those people who are truly professional and businesslike in every sense. Unless you have the right individuals on your sales staff, training will not help.

Do the qualifications I've listed really ensure that you're hiring a potentially good salesperson? I believe they do. One of

> 1. Ambition for self and family.
> 2. Pride in work and accomplishments.
> 3. Good appearance.
> 4. Understanding of and agreement with profit motives.
> 5. Enjoyment of luxury.
> 6. Desire for security.
> 7. Importance of love and family.
> 8. Fear of not obtaining desired goals.
> 9. Enjoyment of prestige.
> 10. Enjoyment of status.

Figure 7. Make a list of the qualifications needed in salespeople.

the most successful salesmen I ever hired had all of these qualities and more. I interviewed him on a Saturday, as I frequently do with new salespeople. The interview time is the first test, to see if the person is willing to work outside a nine-to-five schedule, which is often required in selling. This young man agreed readily and appeared at my office early. After the interview, we walked to the parking lot together. To my surprise, he was driving a brand new, luxurious Lincoln.

"How can you afford this car?" I asked.

"I can't," he retorted. "But that's why I'm here on a Saturday."

Among the salespeople I've hired, the best performers have been those who want the big car, the big home, travel overseas, and all of the luxuries that life has to offer. Ambition and the willingness to work long and hard to achieve that ambition are the most likely signs that you are choosing a person who can be trained to close successfully. This is my reason for listing ambition as the Number 1 quality salespeople should have.

Ambition and the other qualities that I have listed in Figure 7, or that you add to your own list, are doubly important because they are the factors you can use to motivate your sales staff. The salesperson who takes pride in his or her sales record, who wants the money needed to make a good appearance, who has a large mortgage in order to give his or her family a good home, who's main fear is of not obtaining desired goals, and who enjoys prestige, status, security, and luxury is the salesperson who can be most easily and repeatedly motivated. If such a person also believes in the profit-making system that has kept our society strong, he or she will be exceedingly trainable.

Goals and Training

You want your salespeople to have the greatest dreams and ambitions possible. But once they are hired, make sure they are given, or learn to establish, goals that are attainable in the near future. A good way to balance these two extremes is to use a simple goal chart (see Figure 8) early in your training sessions.

You can use any time spans you wish on such a chart: some companies, especially the larger insurance companies, use 10- or even 20-year goals when working with entry-level salespeople. I have found, however, that a maximum of five years is best. To the salesperson, five years is not such a distant time that he or she is unable to visualize it.

In addition to long-term goals, the trainee should set short- and medium-term goals. As you will see in Figure 8, I use six months, one to three years, and five years as target dates on my training charts.

It is also possible to vary the areas in which goals are set. I

Figure 8. A simple goal chart is useful when training salespeople.

GOALS

Area	6 months	1–3 years	5 years
WORK			
MONEY			
POSSESSIONS			
FAMILY/ PERSONAL RELATION- SHIPS			
PERSONAL			

use the same areas in which I look for certain qualities when hiring salespeople: work, money, possessions, family/personal relationships, and personal goals. I want all my salespeople to have and attain high goals in these areas. Their success will make them and my company richer.

When working on the goal charts, whether training several salespeople or one individual, I take each of the first three areas—work, money, and possessions—and go over the goals each salesperson sets for him- or herself. It teaches me a lot and forces the salesperson to think about the direction of his or her career. I then ask the salesperson to complete the family/personal relationships and personal goals areas, but we do not discuss them unless the salesperson requests it. Even if such a discussion is requested, I find it prudent not to give personal advice related to marriages, families, love affairs, and so on. Such advice usually backfires. The purpose of including these areas in my training chart is to be sure that salespeople think about and interrelate all the goals that are important in their lives.

There are many variations of the goal chart that is shown here. Some firms, for example, add an "in your wildest dreams" goal to encourage trainees to think as positively as they can. My own experience has been that trainees respond better to goals that they stand a good chance of achieving. Thus, I choose to limit the time span of the chart to five years. This can be compared to climbing a ladder. I want the salesperson to be able to see the top of the "ladder" (the five-year goal) and also concrete progress up the "rungs" (short- and medium-term goals).

Teach How to Plan Sales and Closings

Once your sales staff is hired, begin your training by teaching the basics of planning for selling and closing. This will not be easy, because most salespeople hate the paperwork and other prerequisites that are inherent in this planning. The secret is to show them what such planning will do to help their sales volume, and how to do it. Then you must follow through to make sure that they continually use their planning.

First, teach the methods for finding prospective buyers, since no salesperson can close sales without a plentiful supply of prospects. These methods will depend on your product or service. If your firm sells storm windows, for example, a salesperson may be taught to prospect simply by walking down a street and observing which homes do not have modern storm windows.

If your product or service is more specialized, show the salesperson how to use directories or mailing lists of names of individuals or firms likely to buy. Teach your staff to note sales made by your competition, where the product is consumed and repeat sales will be made.

After the salesperson has learned to prospect, he or she must be taught the next step—setting up a call schedule. A call schedule is necessary paperwork for trainees and experienced salespeople alike. It helps the salesperson plan and organize sales calls. It keeps the sales manager informed of the salesperson's wherabouts. The form I use with my sales staff is shown in Figure 9. Each salesperson must turn in a weekly travel schedule of firm appointments by Wednesday of the preceding week. This one simple form forces the salesperson to call ahead for appointments and to set up a travel schedule with the number of calls per day that he or she has been instructed to schedule. I train my sales staff, for example, to make four or five calls per day when they are traveling. A glance at this schedule tells me ahead of time whether or not the salespeople are scheduling their calls as instructed.

The schedule also allows me to compare call reports with scheduled calls to make sure that calls were actually made. Over a period of time, the travel schedules tell me how hard an

Figure 9. Completing a call or travel schedule form helps train the salesperson to plan a full and worthwhile trip, with firm appointments.

		INTERNATIONAL GROUP SALESPERSON'S WEEKLY TRAVEL SCHEDULE	
SALESPERSON:		SALESPERSON'S CODE #:	WEEK ENDING:
DATE	ACCOUNT		AREA

individual salesperson is working on specific accounts. Additionally, the current travel schedule helps me quickly locate a salesperson if I have questions.

TEACH SELLING AND CLOSING METHODS

Once the salesperson learns how to find prospects, he or she must next learn how to prepare an individual presentation that will help close the sale.

Teach your salespeople to prepare for each sales call. The first thing I ask my own staff to do is prepare a list of advantages to the prospect of buying our product (see Figure 10). This list should summarize the needs of the prospect for the product or service. The salesperson can then plan his or her presentation to tell the buyer how these needs can be filled.

Help the salesperson prepare at least one presentation. Depending on the type of presentation you know works best in your industry, you might include use of a videotape, a flip chart, samples, and so on. Many sales managers find that, especially with new salespeople, it pays to actually rehearse the presentation. You may make the presentation first, with your salesperson

---

BUYER ADVANTAGES

1. Good income and investment potential.

2. Prestige and security of owning a business.

3. Challenge of working with the public.

Figure 10. A salesperson can prepare for a sales call by making a list of the advantages a prospect will receive when buying a product or service. In this case, the product is a franchise.

playing the role of the prospect. Next, the salesperson should make the presentation, with you acting as the buyer (be sure to raise any objections the actual buyer might).

Be sure that your salespeople read the first seven chapters of this book, as well as any chapters of closing lines that apply to your industry. Or you can take the techniques from those chapters and work them into your instruction.

Be sure to repeat frequently "There is no sale until you ask for the order." You can teach many creative ways to ask for the business, or your staff can learn them by reading this book. But it is essential to keep this phrase constantly before each salesperson—*ask for the order!* Without it, no sale will ever be closed.

THE ROLE OF PAPERWORK

Paperwork is essential in teaching your sales staff to close sales. We have already discussed the paperwork involved in planning (see Figures 9 and 10). However, the most important piece of paper, other than the order itself, is the call report. I recommend that you use call reports for many instructional and selling reasons.

My own favorite call report form is shown in Figure 11. Unlike forms that give only one line per call, this form gives the salesperson room to record what really happened during the call. This allows you to check call reports and quickly determine areas in which the salesperson needs additional training to close sales successfully.

Because this is such an important area, I would like to show you how I use these completed call reports in my own sales training efforts.

Figure 12 shows a call report sent to me by one of my European salesmen. Note the angry tone of the wording on the form. It is easy to understand the salesman's annoyance at the

CLIENT:	
CONTACT:	DATE
AGENCY:	
CONTACT:	SALES PERSON:

Figure 11. A good call report form can provide information that helps the salesperson and shows the sales manager where additional training is needed.

CLIENT:	D & N Services
CONTACT:	C. Lonner
DATE:	10/6/80
AGENCY:	
CONTACT:	SALES PERSON:

Meeting scheduled with client —

Despite an appointment that I had confirmed on 10/5, Lonner was absent when I arrived. (Excuse: with Managing Director at a meeting!)

This is extremely annoying, as Lonner is a man of influence.

Rearranged appointment for early July.

Figure 12. Call reports can warn of poor closing tactics.

Training Salespeople to Close

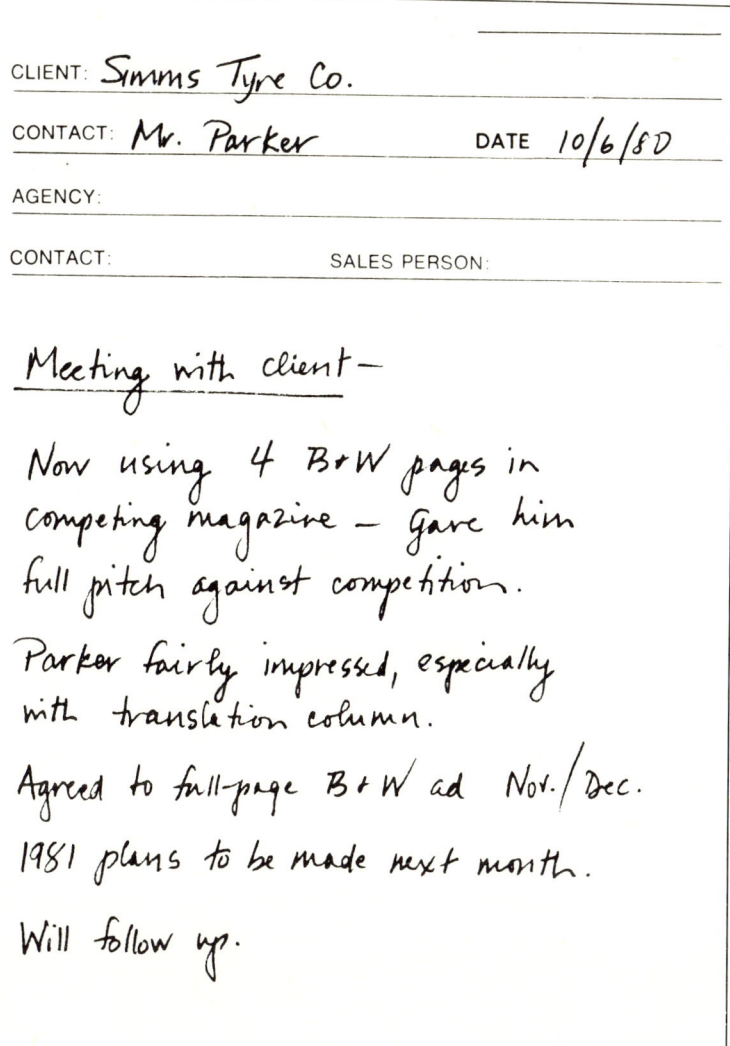

Figure 13. Call reports should tell the sales manager what sort of presentation the salesperson made, what problems were overcome and how, and whether the sale was closed or not.

canceled appointment, yet the tone warned me that I should make sure that this young salesman was not using the same irritated, hostile tone with his prospect.

The same salesman, however, proved what a good presentation he made to another client. By reading the call report shown in Figure 13, I knew that he had successfully overcome buyer objections, had made a presentation that gave us an advantage over the competition, and had closed the sale.

When training your sales staffs to use call report forms, make sure they include what sort of presentation was made, what problems were overcome and how, and whether or not the sale was closed.

I use one additional form for selling, a monthly estimate form. The form shown in Figure 14 is used to estimate the sales of advertising space for our magazines; you can easily adapt it, however, to your own product or service. The purposes of the form are both to make the salesperson think about his or her performance and to provide you, the sales manager, with an advance estimate of sales. When training your sales staff, explain the reasons for using the form and set a specific date when the form must be submitted to you each month. Forms are also used for expense account reports and other accounting functions, but we will not discuss these here.

Prospect cards or loose-leaf prospect books should also be used by salespeople (see Figure 15). This record serves as an up-to-date source of the prospect's name, address, and telephone number. It should include essential facts about the buyer that your salesperson will need to remember. A glance at such information can help the salesperson plan the next call. I teach my salespeople to record facts about the prospect's needs, objections, service details, and so on.

The prospect card really determines how much time your salesperson must spend with the client, how many times the

INTERNATIONAL GROUP MONTHLY ESTIMATE

Month: _____

Salesman: _____

*Return to home office on the 15th of second preceding month
*Call publisher for recap: _____

Scheduled (contracted for or order in hand)	Pages	Promised (better than 75% sure)	Pages	Best possible (better than 50% chance)	Pages

Accounts on open contract

Account	Rate Basis	Insertions Left	Account	Rate Basis	Insertions Left

Salesman's estimate of pages for this month: _____
Use reverse side for additional prospects and/or best possible

Figure 14. Monthly sales estimate forms can be adapted to any product or service and can help the salesperson review his or her own closing efforts.

Figure 15. One side of the prospect/client card can be used to record the buyer's name, address, and phone number as well as the purchase itself (in this case, a schedule of advertising placed). The back of the card can be used to record facts about calls. The salesperson can refer to this information to help prepare presentations for future calls.

CLIENT				PRODUCTION	
FIRM					
ADDRESS		POST CODE		AGENCY	
				ADDRESS	POST CODE
PHONE		TELEX		PHONE	TELEX
NAMES		TITLE		NAME	TITLE
			P.A.L.		
PRODUCTS				SCHEDULE DATE:	

	JAN	FEB	MAR	APR	MAY	JUNE	JULY	AUG	SEPT	OCT	NOV	DEC

Call Date	Call Details

client has been called on, and his or her buying habits. It is a profile that tells your salesperson how to behave with the prospect and helps in closing future sales—assuming you have taught the ways to use the card.

It is also important to train your sales staff to complete all paperwork after normal business hours. The salesperson can earn an exceptional amount of money and must expect to work more hours than a normal work week. Conventional working hours should be used by the salesperson exclusively to sell and close sales.

Teach Good Letter Writing, Too

Some of your salespeople may already know how to write good sales letters. Many do not. Some of the principles can be taught by showing them the well-written letters in Appendix A. But also review with them the following basic guidelines:

1. Start the letter with a statement, a question, or an offer that will help the buyer. If the salesperson has nothing of value for the prospect, he or she should not be writing a letter.
2. Explain the facts quickly and concisely. Good sales letters are short but complete.
3. Ask for the order in sales letters, as well as on personal calls.
4. Follow up sales letters with a telephone call to get the answer.

Measuring Performance

A part of the training you give your sales staff should be a session on evaluating their work. Show the salesperson forms and records you or your accounting department uses to measure performance. Explain how his or her quota is determined, as well as how commissions are paid. A short session of this sort not only will help to motivate your salespeople but will help them realize how their own paperwork fits into the overall selling picture.

A Sample Training Curriculum

All these facts are useful in training your sales staff. For a more structured approach, however, you may wish to use my three-day training curriculum. This shows you, step-by-step, how I train each new member of my sales staff.

Day 1: Home Office
9:00–10:00 A.M.: An introductory session in my office, including a discussion of the products to be sold and the salesperson's territory, including its overall challenges and problems.
10:00–11:00 A.M.: Time for the salesperson to examine product samples, promotional literature, and so on.
11:00–Noon: Discussion of the products and how they can best be presented to prospects.
Noon–2:00 P.M.: Lunch with other staff members. An informal question and answer session is encouraged.
2:00–4:00 P.M.: Instruction in my techniques for product presentation, closing, paperwork, and so on.
4:00–5:00 P.M.: Salesperson is instructed to write out a "typical" sales call, including all possible prospect objections and his or her responses to such objections, to be used on Day 2 (see Figure 16).

Day 2: Home Office/Field Work
9:00–12:00 A.M.: We practice selling, using the role-playing scenario prepared by the salesperson. First, the new salesperson takes the part of the buyer and I demonstrate my selling and closing techniques as if I were the salesperson. Next, I assume the role of the buyer and raise objections to see if the salesperson has learned to handle them.

Figure 16. The salesperson can prepare a typical sales call dialogue.

Salesperson Good morning, Mr. Prospect. Thanks for taking the time to let me tell you about *World Construction's* new rate protection plan.

Prospect I need some rate protection—your rates have increased twice in the past year!

Salesperson That's exactly why this plan was developed—to protect our regular advertisers, such as yourself. Have you read the literature we sent you explaining the plan?

Prospect I don't have time to read that stuff.

Salesperson Let me explain it quickly to you, then. All of the space you schedule for next year will be billed at this year's price, provided your schedule is received by October 15.

Prospect Does that mean your rates are going up again?

Salesperson It's inevitable that all magazine rates will go up because of paper and postage cost increases. But you can avoid any of these increases when you advertise with us.

Prospect I'm not sure what my schedule will be next year.

Salesperson That's why I'm here today. Because we can save you money, we believe you'll get the most for your advertising dollar by deciding to take advantage of our offer. Are you planning to increase your overall schedule next year?

Prospect We are thinking about it. With the U.S. economy so poor, exports looks like the only way.

Salesperson This plan will let you increase your schedule without the price increases you'd have to pay elsewhere. May I suggest MLO spread ads in each issue?

Prospect What would that cost?

Salesperson (figuring on pad) That would give you a 24 x rate—only $1,860 per page.

Prospect That's not too bad.

Salesperson If you remind your agency of the savings, I'm sure they will issue the insertion order before October 15.

1:00–4:00 P.M.: The new salesperson makes a local call with an established member of the sales staff to observe how another salesperson uses my selling and closing techniques.

Day 3: In the Field
9:00 A.M.–10:00 P.M.: The salesperson and I make joint calls on at least four prospects in his or her territory, including a lunch and a dinner call. The salesperson makes the presentation but observes how I handle objections and close if he or she is unable to do so.

This simple curriculum can be adapted for use with any product or service. Its success in training salespeople depends on how you use it.

For the introductory sessions, be sure to have in the training room an adequate supply of product samples, promotional literature, advertisements you have used, and forms the salesperson will be required to use. If the trainee is replacing another salesperson, as opposed to filling a newly created position, have all pertinent records available. These should include sales records, prospect cards, correspondence, and so on. Use role-playing and other methods that require the salesperson to simulate his or her performance in the field.

On the second day, be sure that the new salesperson makes calls with a truly competent member of your sales staff, to ensure the best learning experience.

On the third day, let the new salesperson sell. Take part only when it is obvious that your salesperson has a problem he or she doesn't know how to handle.

9

Teaching to close by example

Once your salesperson has received basic training, he or she can always use further instruction in actual closing. No method really works as well as observing how a top-quality salesperson who already knows the product and the industry closes sales. But teaching how to close by example is not as simple as it sounds.

PRACTICE CLOSING BEFORE THE CALL

Just as I suggested the use of role-playing for initial training, I suggest you and your salesperson practice making the close prior to any joint sales call. Begin such a practice session with a quick analysis of the prospect, if you or the salesperson know the individual:

What does the buyer want and need most?
What are his or her hang-ups, likes, dislikes?
How can the buyer be most easily approached?
What will it take to close the sale?

In your practice session, have the salesperson plan the entire preparation, just as he or she will do when you're making an actual sales call together. The salesperson should give you a prospect card and/or prospect dossier for each call that will be made. Do your own prospect research to be sure the salesperson is doing his or her homework well.

Find a third party, one the salesperson doesn't know, to play the role of the prospective buyer. Be sure this person doesn't get carried away and ask questions no real prospect would ask. Your goal is to teach your salespeople how to close a sale not to embarrass them.

As the salesperson begins the practice call, take notes, stop and explain why a technique will or will not work, and interject comments. In other words, put in whatever constructive advice you can during the practice session; you won't be able to do this on real sales calls, of course.

Study your salesperson's reaction to your comments. Did he or she get rattled? Did he lose his place or train of thought? Did she just fall into the stream of action and work with you, as a team? Make notes on these reactions and discuss both the pluses and minuses with your salesperson.

Making the Joint Call

After these practice sessions have been completed, it is time to make joint calls in the field. The rules are not the same as during practice sessions.

Your salesperson will understand that he or she is being observed during your joint calls. Make sure he or she also knows that you are going along to learn firsthand about the territory and to help close sales whenever necessary.

The salesperson must do all of the planning for the joint sales calls; be very careful not to interfere in this area. Be prepared to keep whatever schedule the salesperson would normally complete, and do not expect to have dinners or other entertainments arranged mainly for your benefit rather than to close a sale.

With my own sales staffs, I like to leave everything to them. It lets me judge many aspects of their performance. Joint calls also provide a means of continued training.

Plan to use an evaluation form for every joint call made. (Naturally, you will not complete this form during the sales call nor in the presence of the salesperson.) To use the sample form shown in Figure 17, circle the rating level in each area of performance. The overall rating is the total of the numbers circled, with a maximum score of 100. Use the comments section to record your observations of the salesperson's performance. Such observations are quite valuable for comparison when you later evaluate a salesperson's growth.

Before the joint call is made, decide whether you will be an observer, whether you will help the salesperson close a sale, or whether you will do both.

If you plan to observe only, control your own sales enthusiasm and listen to your salesperson. Make mental notes so that you can complete the evaluation form later. Even if you plan only to observe, intercede if your salesperson gets off the track. But don't close a sale if your only role on a joint call is to observe. Such a call will best serve as a courtesy call, with your salesperson closing later.

Joint calls can be used to close effectively as well as to provide training. In this case, have your salesperson explain to the prospective client that you are coming along on the call to offer the client more beneficial information, that as sales manager, you travel widely and have more firsthand information about the marketplace. This is especially effective if you visit markets the prospect does not. When you meet the prospect, put all your best selling and closing techniques or those in Chapters 1–7 to work. This both sets an example for your salesperson and also gives you an opportunity to keep your hand in selling.

Work with your salesperson before the call to be sure that he or she can occasionally add something to your presentation. This will help build the salesperson's image in the prospect's eyes and benefit him or her on future calls.

In many cases, it is possible to create a dialogue by having your salesperson ask you if a copy of some market research

Figure 17. Use this kind of form for each joint call you make.

SALESPERSON EVALUATION FORM

Call Date_____

Salesperson_____

Client/Agency_____

Circle rating, with 10 as best

Performance

Self-confidence	10	9	8	7	6	5	4	3	2	1
Appearance	10	9	8	7	6	5	4	3	2	1
Preparation	10	9	8	7	6	5	4	3	2	1
Opening	10	9	8	7	6	5	4	3	2	1
Organization	10	9	8	7	6	5	4	3	2	1
Presentation	10	9	8	7	6	5	4	3	2	1
Product/Service Knowledge	10	9	8	7	6	5	4	3	2	1
Handling of Objections	10	9	8	7	6	5	4	3	2	1
Enthusiasm	10	9	8	7	6	5	4	3	2	1
Closing Skill	10	9	8	7	6	5	4	3	2	1

Overall Rating_____

Comments:

(which you may have been discussing) can be sent to the prospect free of charge. When you say yes, you make the salesperson look good for requesting data of interest to the buyer. Another approach is for the salesperson to ask the prospect if he or she would like to have a copy of this market research. Almost always, the prospect will respond with a resounding yes, setting the scene for a positive close. Once the prospect starts saying that magic word *yes*, your chances of closing the sale successfully will climb.

As sales manager, you can speed the actual closing at this point by telling the prospect what your product can do to benefit him or her. You can make a special price or service offer that the salesperson theoretically could not make. Such interplay has a strong positive effect on the prospect. The buyer will believe he or she is getting more because you are there, and the sale will be closed.

You can also reverse this tactic on joint calls to achieve the same results. In this scenario, the salesperson offers something extra, such as a special market research study or a discount, saying he or she heard you talk about the service on an earlier call and wants to be sure that this client also receives the extra.

Still another approach is for you to remind the salesperson at the point he or she offers an extra that only one such offer will be made on this trip. The following example will show you how well prospects respond to what I call "the only one" principle.

Recently, I made a joint call with a midwestern salesman on my staff. After the presentation, which included a discussion of readers' response to our magazine, the salesman made a suggestion. "Let's do a 'did-you-buy' study for your company," he said to the advertiser. "That's the best way to measure response to both our magazine and your ad. It should help you decide whether to change your ad this year."

"That's fine, Bob," I told him, breaking into the conversation. "But remember you're allowed only one free 'did-you-buy' study in your territory this quarter."

"I want Mr. X's company to have it," the salesman told me. "I know you'll put it to good use," he said to the advertiser.

Naturally, the advertiser was eager to accept the *only* survey offered, and he also bought a nice schedule of advertising.

The same principle can be used during the selling process. This same salesman said to an advertiser, "I'd like to offer you the advertising position next to the opening of this important show report—every reader will see that page and only one advertiser can be located there."

Of course, the sale was quickly closed.

Evaluating Sales Training from Joint Calls

Good sales managers never stop evaluating how their examples affect their sales staff. Look regularly for key factors during calls that tell you whether continued training has been successful:

- Does the salesperson prepare adequately for each call?
- Does the salesperson show confidence without being cocky?
- Does the salesperson listen to and understand the prospect?
- Is the salesperson's mind organized so that he or she doesn't digress or forget the point of the call?
- Does the salesperson show enthusiasm?
- Is the salesperson pleasant and positive when making calls?
- Does the salesperson know his or her product well?
- Does the salesperson know *when* to close?
- Does the salesperson know *how* to close?

The effectiveness of sales training is as much a reflection on you as on your salesperson. The sales manager must set an example by acting as a successful salesperson and being able to transfer this success and knowledge to his or her sales staff. As a sales manager, your work is cut out for you. But the rewards are more than monetary.

10

What to do with the salesperson who can't close

Every experienced sales manager has had salespeople who do everything right—until it is time to close. Some of these people do occasionally close sales because prospects are so anxious to buy the product or service that the sales close themselves. Others close without realizing they are doing so. In the latter case, the salesperson is comparable to a good actor who suffers from stage fright but is really an accomplished performer. Both the actor and the salesperson need help.

Danger Signs That Signal Closing Failure

To help the salesperson who can't close, begin by recognizing the danger signs. If your salesperson shows four or more of the following traits, he or she most certainly has problems closing:

- Never or seldom asks the sales manager to make joint calls.
- Seldom brings in new accounts or new divisions of present accounts.
- Is difficult to find if you have questions; no travel schedule is available.
- Always has many excuses for the lack of new business, such as blaming competition or some aspect of the product.

- Completes more than three times as many call reports as sales.
- Sells less than the volume in comparable territories.
- Has lower volume than his or her predecessor.
- Has lower volume than the competitor's salesperson in the same territory.

THE REASONS BEHIND CLOSING FAILURES

The danger signs warn you that a salesperson is unable to close. But in order to help this person, you must understand the reasons behind the closing failures.

The first danger sign, when a salesperson seldom or never asks you to make joint sales calls, may mean that this person has trouble asking for help. What are the reasons? Salespeople may be afraid to admit they have problems; they may think they will lose the job or have to learn an entirely new sales presentation. Salespeople who never ask for help are, in other words, afraid of rocking the boat. You can work on this problem by inviting yourself on joint calls.

What about the salesperson who seldom or never brings in a new account or cannot even bring in business from other divisions of a current account? If old business remains fairly stable, this probably means that the salesperson is good at providing service but doesn't know enough about selling or closing. Additional training and joint calls are initial steps in working with this type of salesperson.

Salespeople sometimes become difficult to find when they're having trouble closing simply because they don't want to face the sales manager or their closing problems. When a salesperson "hides" from me by not leaving travel schedules, not calling the office regularly, and so on, I know that he or she needs my help immediately.

Most salespeople make excuses to justify either temporary or ongoing lack of business. They may blame the competition, the economy, the time of year, the product, or any of a hundred other factors. The truth usually is that they need help learning to close.

Another important danger sign is when the number of call reports a salesperson turns in is three or more times the number of actual sales. Often this indicates that calls were not well handled. In some cases, phony call reports may be turned in to cover up closing problems that need your attention.

Sales volume is also a key indicator. You know help is needed when your salesperson's volume drops compared with the volume of salespeople in other territories or the performance of your competitor's salesperson in the same territory. Reasons for such volume drops may include personal problems or a change in selling and closing techniques.

Breaking "Closing Block"

Whatever the reasons for the failure to close, your salesperson needs help in breaking "closing block." The first approach is simply to repeat the closing lessons outlined earlier in this book, to refresh the salesperson's memory.

"Even good salespeople grow stale with their closings," one sales manager recently reminded me. "They get tired of using the same closings, even though they work. They cut them short or take the sizzle out and don't even realize what they've done."

A quick refresher course in the basics of closing will usually solve this problem. One of the most effective ways to achieve this is to demonstrate good closing methods during joint sales calls. Also be sure to remind the salesperson frequently how important closing is. One sales manager put specially made posters in each salesperson's office, which read: "No sale can be made till you ask for the order."

To sell a product, the salesperson must ask for the order repeatedly and in different ways throughout a sales call. To sell the importance of closing, you must repeatedly ask your salespeople to close.

Gimmicks can also be used to help break closing blocks. One of

What to Do with the Salesperson Who Can't Close

the best of these is to tape-record a call. Use a long-length cassette so that the salesperson does not need to change it during a call. The recorder should be carried in the salesperson's briefcase or sample case and turned on before the call begins so that the prospect doesn't know the meeting is being recorded. If you are making a joint call, you may want to make the recording without warning the salesperson or the prospect.

The purpose of the recording is not to shame the salesperson but to let him or her listen to closing mistakes at leisure after the call. If you have interceded to help close the sale, the positive moves you made can also be analyzed. With such a recording, you and the salesperson can go over the call again and again, discussing good and weak steps in the selling and closing. Practice or role-playing sessions can be recorded and discussed in the same way.

After listening to some tapes with your salespeople, suggest that they continue to make and analyze tapes on their own. This lets them evaluate their selling and closing techniques without feeling pressured by your presence.

Use of order pads, handwritten messages on note pads, and other closing gimmicks outlined in the first seven chapters of this book should be reviewed and put into action whenever a closing block occurs.

Good-guy/bad-guy routines can also help salespeople overcome closing blocks. These are joint calls in which you and your salesperson each assume either the "white hat good guy" or "black hat bad guy" role.

For example, the two of you may call on an account that the salesperson has tried unsuccessfully to close many times. Your salesperson (in this case, the bad guy) makes the standard presentation. Then you, the good guy, offer something extra and close the sale. Or you can be the bad guy, with the salesperson "persuading" you to make a special offer and closing in top good-guy fashion.

Instructing others can help salespeople overcome closing difficulties, too. Whenever I have a salesperson who is experiencing such difficulties, I ask him or her to prepare a training session to teach new salespeople how to close. Psychologically, this helps the salesperson overcome his or her closing block. It also forces a review of closing techniques without your having to play a heavy role.

Another way to help salespeople beat closing blocks is to emphasize techniques that involve getting the prospect to agree with something—preferably many things—since this sets the scene to close. Encourage creativity in using these techniques.

One of my most difficult prospects when I was a salesman was a man who would never agree—in fact, he seldom said anything. During several calls, I tried to get him to say something positive, but with no results.

Finally, an idea hit me. During the middle of my presentation, I looked at the window behind him and announced "God, Hal, it looks like it's going to snow." He immediately responded with "What in the hell are you talking about; it's the middle of summer?"

My retort was that I didn't believe it would actually snow, but if you were just looking at the picture of the sky, which was very cloudy, with the wind blowing in the streets, it did look like one of those wintry days when snow would soon be coming. Hal took a look outside, partially because he must have thought I was crazy to interrupt a sales representation with such a comment. He came back with the reply, "Yes, it really does look like that kind of day."

Not only had I gotten him to say something, I had even managed to get him to use the magic word *yes*. Knowing it was part of his vocabulary and knowing that he could use it, all I had to do then was to alter my presentation to get him to speak up.

This method can be used over and over again, and the sales manager should show the salesperson how to do this on a sales

What to Do with the Salesperson Who Can't Close

call. The question asked by the salesperson need not be about the weather; it can be about any subject. The point is to make the prospect say something, preferably yes.

OVERCOMING OBJECTIONS

If a salesperson is having problems closing, chances are great that he or she is not handling objections correctly. You can help solve this problem by working with the salesperson. Begin by telling the salesperson to list every objection to buying your product or service he or she has ever heard.

A typical list might include:

- I like your product, but my boss wants to buy from another supplier.
- Our company can get this cheaper from someone else.
- We don't need your product.
- Your prices are too high.
- We want to spend the money on something else.
- We have no budget for your product.
- We might be in the market for your product next year.
- We've surveyed our managers, and they prefer a different brand.
- We are completely satisfied with our present supplier and don't want to change.
- We want to think about it.
- Your product is too new; it hasn't been tested enough.
- Your product is too old and out of date.
- The economy is bad, and management wants us to cut back.
- I don't have the time to see you.
- You're too late; we've already decided to buy another brand.
- Your service wasn't good the last time we bought from you.

Be sure your salesperson completes his or her own list, then combine it with my list. The next step is to help the salesperson learn to answer these objections in a way that moves toward a successful close. Don't make the mistake of telling your salesperson to do this alone—it won't work!

No matter how time consuming, work out all answers that overcome each objection on the salesperson's list. Write these down or dictate them as you and the salesperson come up with one, two, or more answers. Eventually, you should have a written or typed list of objections and appropriate answers. The salesperson can study these and use the answers when selling.

For example, a prospect may say, "I don't have time to see you." From experience, you know that this objection can be handled successfully in several ways. The salesperson may reply, "I realize how busy you are, and I don't want to take up any of your time today. I would appreciate it if I could leave our new price lists for you and make an appointment to explain our discount system some day next week when you have more time."

Or the prospect may object saying he or she prefers a competitor's products. In this case, the salesperson must reverse the situation. He or she can say, "I know you're pleased with your current supplier, but I believe we have some services no one else can offer if you'll give us a try with one order."

It is important for you as sales manager to continually remind the salesperson not to accept objections but to deal with them. Not too long ago, I was reading call reports from a salesman who reported on nothing but prospect objections but made no suggestions for dealing with these. Finally, I came to a call report that said, "The prospect seems married to the XYZ Company." "Arrange for a divorce," I wrote across the report and mailed it back to the rep.

As sales manager, also be prepared to listen to your salespeople and to the objections they receive in the field. Practice overcoming the objections, using the list the rep has put together.

When to Call It Quits

A good sales manager will try to help salespeople who are having problems. But what if, after receiving a lot of help, the salesperson still cannot close? Dismissal is the only answer. And how much time should you put into helping nonclosers before you get rid of them?

Look at the past selling record as the first guideline. If the salesperson was once good at closing, be willing to put more time and effort into helping. Search for problem areas. These are most likely to include:

- Personal problems that prevent concentration. Since you should not become involved here, you may wish to recommend professional counseling.
- A change in selling techniques, such as taking shortcuts in a presentation. These problems can be overcome by going back to the original presentation.
- A change in the market due to the economy, new competition, greater buyer sophistication, and so on. Here, a new presentation should be put together that will let the salesperson close successfully.

Evaluate current problems of the salesperson having difficulty and the potential for helping him or her overcome these problems. If the investment of a week or two will provide you with a competent salesperson, invest that time.

Admit failure when deep inside you know a salesperson cannot be salvaged fairly quickly. Just the shock of change may force an incompetent salesperson to improve or to change his or her career path.

III

250 SUCCESSFUL CLOSING LINES

Having learned the basics of closing, you will find it useful to have a good supply of proven closing lines. Also remember that closing lines can and should be used throughout the presentation, from beginning to end. These lines won't close the sale on their own, of course. But when worked into a sound presentation, they can help you close that sale.

In addition, a good closing line can help you avoid a close I actually heard a salesman make not too long ago. "You wouldn't want to buy a page in our [media selection] magazine, would you?" he asked me. He made it very easy for me to reply, "No, I wouldn't," which is the reply I made.

11

Fifty closing lines that work in retail selling

1. I have just one (black dress, watchband, etc.) left in that model.
2. Do you like the (blue, green, etc.) one best?
3. I find these to be the most comfortable (shoes, chairs, etc.) made.
4. Would you like to use our budget plan to pay for that?
5. You've made a good choice—that's an excellent quality (watch, appliance, etc.).
6. Would you like to have it delivered?
7. Would you like to take it with you?
8. We have a special with a second (bottle, jar, etc.) for half price.
9. We can guarantee the (appliance, watch, etc.) for a year rather than the usual 90 days with this model.
10. Would you like me to order the (title, color, size, etc.) that you like best?
11. Would a (heavy-duty, light-weight, automatic, etc.) model be best for you?
12. This (dress, appliance, etc.) is just a bit more expensive, but it's been proven to last nearly twice as long as the other model.

13. With inflation still going up, buying a (car, appliance, etc.) will save you money in a very short time.
14. With the current recession, you can save money with this energy-saving model.
15. Don't you agree that this model has the most features?
16. Would you like a dozen, to take advantage of getting the thirteenth (pair, unit, etc.) free?
17. Would you like the low-cost service contract to go along with the (television, mixer, heater, etc.)?
18. It may not fit, but since it's the only one, why not try it on?
19. Would you like us to bill you after the first of the month for that, rather than now?
20. The manufacturer isn't making (bracelets, rings, crystal, etc.) of that quality now. This may be your only chance to have one.
21. Would you like to sign up for the three free lessons available with that (sewing machine, piano, etc.)?
22. I believe I can find the deluxe model for you at the same cost. Let me check with shipping.
23. Would you like to try on a nice (blouse, shirt, etc.) with that (suit, coat, etc.) to see how smart it looks?
24. This is the last shipment we'll receive before the price goes up.
25. We can guarantee this low price for six weeks if you sign the order today.
26. Is this what you wanted?
27. Do you want full or partial (car, life, home owner, etc.) insurance coverage?
28. If you take it with you today, you can have a ten-day free trial period.
29. (Watches, diamonds, silverware) are really a good investment as well as a good purchase in times like these.
30. Do you prefer the model with or without (snaps, decoration, an automatic switch, etc.)?

Fifty Closing Lines That Work in Retail Selling

31. Would you like it gift wrapped?
32. You can start with the basic set and add to it when you need more (silverware, pans, crystal, etc.).
33. Can you afford ($10, $20, $30) a month?
34. Why wait when you can enjoy your (car, fur coat, etc.) now?
35. I can hold it till this afternoon if you like—this model is selling quickly, and I don't want you to miss out.
36. The larger size saves you 30 percent per (ounce, pound, etc.).
37. Someone with good taste should have this (coat, dress, picture, etc.). I'll make you a good price on it.
38. We're only offering this low price to (charge, good, repeat, etc.) customers.
39. If you ever have a problem with the (catch, handle, etc.), bring it back to me and I'll take care of it.
40. Would you like a (case, protective cover, mat, etc.) to go with the (clock, toaster, typewriter, etc.)?
41. That model has been discontinued, but I have one of the new, improved models left.
42. Have you decided which (tire, appliance, etc.) you like best?
43. This is the same model that (the mayor, the president, Jane Fonda, etc.) uses.
44. Would you like to take advantage of the 5 percent cash discount?
45. Which (flowers, candy, liquor, etc.) will your (wife, girl, mother, etc.) prefer?
46. Why not place a standing order to make sure you don't run out?
47. You're making the right decision. This is the best (appliance, jewelry, etc.) made for that price.
48. If you want to save (time, money, effort, etc.), this is the product that will help you do it.
49. Do you want a humorous or serious (card, gift, etc.)?
50. How many would you like?

12

Fifty closing lines that work in industrial selling

1. This product will help you stay ahead of your competition. How many would you like?
2. Would you like to place a standing order to be sure your supply is never interrupted?
3. Would you like us to warehouse it for you and ship it as you need it?
4. (Writing on order pad) Will a gross be enough?
5. We can offer you a guaranteed price for three months if your order is placed today.
6. There's been a shortage of that product, but I can try to get you a case. May I call our shipping office collect to check on availability?
7. Which one will perform best with your machines?
8. Would you like us to bill you after the first of the year, rather than next month?
9. Do you have the (power, guts, balls, etc.) to sign this order?
10. Do you plan to place your order today?
11. Do you prefer a heavy-duty, long-lasting model or a lightweight economical unit?
12. If you place your six-month order today, you'll save on the inflation-caused price increases that are bound to be ahead.

Fifty Closing Lines That Work in Industrial Selling 119

13. How would you like these shipped—by air or regular freight?
14. Do you think that this model has the best features for your use?
15. Would you like our economical service contract to go with the machine?
16. This is the last one you'll be able to get of this quality.
17. Would you like to try it in your (shop, office, factory, etc.) for 30 days at no cost to you?
18. Would you like to send your operators to our training school, or would you prefer to have an instructor teach them in your own (office, factory, shop, etc.)?
19. This will be the last shipment before the price goes up, so you may want to order more.
20. (Machines, products, etc.) like these are really an investment when the inflation rate climbs.
21. Would you prefer the model with or without the (automatic controls, oversize engine, etc.)?
22. Would you like these products shipped in reusable crates to help cut your own shipment costs?
23. You can start wtih the basic low-cost (computer, unit, etc.) and add (terminals, subunits, etc.) as you want.
24. Why wait, when this (machine, computer, etc.) can cut your costs now?
25. I can reserve your (computer, machine, etc.) this week, before production is stopped for the (summer, Christmas, etc.) vacation period.
26. We're only giving this special price to (new, good, repeat, etc.) customers.
27. Would you like the (printout unit, automatic monitor, etc.) to go with the machine?
28. That model has been discontinued, but I have a heavy-duty model at the same price.
29. This is the same model (GM, Exxon, IBM, etc.) uses.

30. You're making the right decision. This is the best (computer, tire, machine, etc.) made for that price.
31. If you want to increase production, this is the machine that will help you do it.
32. If I make you a really special price, can you sign the order today?
33. Can we help your production by shipping you one of these machines?
34. Are you thoroughly convinced that you need this product?
35. Remember, if you order today, it will take you (six weeks, three months, etc.) to receive it.
36. You've bought the product; what you need now is to tie a ribbon around it with an extra (cover, unit, etc.).
37. You've invested a lot in your operation, and this purchase will help you make that investment pay off.
38. Are you aware of the inroads your competitor has already made using this product?
39. This purchase is like building a good foundation for a new house—it will help make your operation a sound one.
40. Can I reserve a shipment for you?
41. Would one order from (10, 100, etc.) prospective buyers more than pay for this new machine?
42. Let us do a "did-you-buy" study to show you how much our product can help your production.
43. Do you realize that this service can help you in the export market, which has greater profits than the domestic market?
44. Have you ever compared the cost of our product with the cost of what you're using now?
45. The cost of this product is less than the cost of the business lost from using your current model.
46. What will you try to accomplish with this (product, service, etc.)?
47. Think of this order as an investment, not an expense.
48. Every company has a contingency fund for something special.

49. This automated machine will save you money when you consider increasing labor union wages.
50. You've bought our service, so we'll offer your subsidiaries the same service for half the price.

13

Fifty closing lines that work in wholesale sales

1. We can warehouse these special-price goods for you and drop ship.
2. Our products are guaranteed to increase your sales.
3. We'll provide a merchandising package along with the products.
4. Sell this line and you'll be ahead of your competition.
5. If you place a standing order, we'll guarantee the price for the next six months.
6. Would you like to cut your selling costs? Our program for advertising this line will do it.
7. We expect a shortage of (copper, oil products, etc.), but you can be sure your customers are supplied by ordering now.
8. We can invoice you next month rather than this month if you'd prefer.
9. Which product line do you prefer?
10. Infation will push up prices of this line soon. If you buy now, you can hold your costs steady.
11. (Pulling out order pad) Will six boxes be enough?
12. How would you like these shipped—by rail or truck?
13. Will your customers prefer the solid state or the less expensive model?

14. Are you the one who makes the buying decision?
15. Do you plan to add this line to your stock now?
16. Does this model have all the features your customers want?
17. Would you like to take advantage of our cooperative advertising plan to cut your marketing costs?
18. Your customers won't be able to buy products of this quality once this supply is gone.
19. Would you like to stock this line on a trial basis for 30 days?
20. This is the last week before a major price increase, so you may want to increase your order.
21. Merchandise like this is really an investment with our current inflation rate.
22. Why wait, when consumers are increasing their purchases of this product now?
23. We're only offering this special price to (new, good, repeat, etc.) customers.
24. A display unit of (batteries, bulbs, cords, etc.) placed near your new stock of (radios, lamps, appliances, etc.) could provide you with some good add-on sales.
25. This is the same line featured by (Saks, Marshall Field, Lord & Taylor, etc.).
26. You're making the right decision. Your sales will be good with this line.
27. If you want to increase your sales by 30 percent, this is the line that can help you do it.
28. If I give you an extra 5 percent discount, can you sign the order today?
29. Can we help you increase your sales by shipping you a display unit with a gross of (radios, pens, etc.)?
30. Remember that if you order today it will be (six weeks, three months, etc.) until you have it on the floor for your (Christmas, back-to-school, etc.) buyers.
31. You've bought your main line of (radios, mixers, etc.); now you need to make it a complete package with a side display of (batteries, bowls, etc.).

32. You've invested a lot in your store, and carrying this line of goods will help you make that investment pay off.
33. Do you know how many gross of these products your competitor sells each (week, month, etc.)?
34. Are you thoroughly convinced that your customers will buy this product?
35. If you take a (dozen, case, gross, etc.), we'll supply an easy-show display unit free.
36. Are you aware of the inroads your competition has already made in the market by selling this product?
37. Can I reserve a (case, dozen, gross, etc.) for you?
38. Have you compared the cost of our line with the cost of what you're selling now?
39. What sales goal will you try to reach with this line of goods?
40. Think of this order as an investment rather than an expense.
41. I have just one (case, gross, dozen, etc.) left in that style.
42. I'm really not trying to sell you; I'm trying to help you.
43. When you sign this order today, you'll get six new products free, to test the market for us.
44. When you order this line, we'll do a buyer-response survey for you free.
45. Many of our customers find they can take a 150 percent markup on this line rather than the standard 100 percent and still have good market response.
46. This product will save on total selling cost because it's prepackaged.
47. (With order pad in hand) Tell me how many you'd like.
48. You'll never have a price this low—the production change will be made next week.
49. Your customers can special-order options after looking at the basic (car, camper, etc.), and we'll deliver promptly.
50. If you carry this line now, we'll guarantee you exclusive rights within the city.

14

Fifty closing lines that work when selling intangibles

1. I'm not trying to sell you anything; I'm trying to help you.
2. Make your management aware of your knowledge by recommending our service.
3. What would you do if you suddenly found you couldn't obtain this service?
4. How do you know you're getting the best service now?
5. The cost of poor service is greater than the cost of our solving your service problems.
6. Our service can help you (lose weight, progress in your job, quit smoking, etc.).
7. If you don't come back after the first visit, we'll refund the price of your (lesson, treatment, etc.).
8. You can save 30 percent by signing up for a series of (treatments, lessons, etc.).
9. Considering the current shortage of (teachers, repairmen, etc.) for this area, you're getting a real bargain.
10. Would you like (6, 12, 18, etc.) (lessons, treatments, etc.), or would you prefer (12, 18, 30)?
11. We can guarantee this low price for six months if you sign up today.

12. Which (program, class, treatment, etc.) is best for your needs?
13. Would you like to use our convenient budget plan?
14. Do you have the authority to sign the order, or must you take it to your boss?
15. Are you convinced that these (treatments, lessons, etc.) can do the job for you?
16. Would you like our low-cost renewal guarantee with your contract?
17. This is the last series of (lessons, treatments, etc.) that will be given this year.
18. You can renew this contract for less than (47 cents, 62 cents, etc.) a day.
19. Would you like to try a sample (lesson, treatment, etc.) at no cost to you?
20. Would you like to schedule (lessons, treatments, etc.) in our offices, or would you prefer that a (tutor, masseur, etc.) visit you?
21. There's only one vacancy left in this (class, schedule, etc.).
22. These (classes, treatments, insurance policies, etc.) are really an investment.
23. You can start with the low-cost basic service and add services as you desire.
24. Why wait, when this (class, treatment, etc.) can help you accomplish what you want now?
25. I can reserve your place in this (class, schedule, issue, etc.) if you give the O.K. now.
26. We're only giving this special price to (new, good, credit, repeat, etc.) customers.
27. Would you like the (books, lotion, etc.) to go with the (lessons, treatments, etc.)?
28. Those (classes, treatments, etc.) have been discontinued, but we have a better (teacher, therapist, etc.) starting a new series next week.

Fifty Closing Lines That Work When Selling Intangibles

29. These are the same (classes, treatments, etc.) that helped (your brother, the mayor, etc.).
30. You're making the right decision. This is the best (class, treatment, policy, service, etc.) for your purpose.
31. If I make you a really special price, can you sign the order now?
32. Remember, if you start today it will take (six weeks, ten weeks, three months, etc.) to (lose ten pounds, learn French, etc.).
33. If you want to (learn, earn, do, etc.) more, this is the (class, treatment, etc.) that will help you do it.
34. You've bought our service, so we'll offer you the same service for your (wife, friend, child, etc.) at half price.
35. This service is an investment that will pay off in (lost weight, more knowledge, greater security, etc.).
36. Let us do a before-and-after study to show you how this (class, treatment, etc.) has improved you.
37. Do you realize that this (class, treatment, etc.) can help you with your job as well as in your personal life?
38. Have you ever compared the cost of our (class, policy, service, etc.) with the cost of what you're using now?
39. Imagine how good you'll feel about yourself once you've finished this (class, treatment, etc.)?
40. Think of this purchase as an investment in yourself.
41. This (class, treatment, policy, service, etc.) is a little more expensive, but its extra features make it worth it.
42. Which (treatments, classes, etc.) would be best for you?
43. I believe I can persuade the (teacher, publisher, etc.) to give you (extra attention, a special ad position, etc.) at no extra cost. Can I place a collect call to check?
44. Do you want full or partial (insurance coverage, security protection, etc.)?
45. A gift certificate is an ideal answer for (business, Christmas, etc.) giving.

46. Can you afford ($5, $10, $20, etc.) a week?
47. The longer series of (classes, treatments, etc.) saves you 25 percent.
48. Would your (family, business, etc.) be protected if you (died, got sick, lost your job, etc.) tomorrow?
49. Would you like to take advantage of the 5 percent cash discount?
50. Will this be cash or charge?

15

Fifty closing lines that work when selling internationally

1. With the low value of the dollar, your cost has been lowered by more than 20 percent.
2. I'm not trying to sell you anything; I'm going to help you with an unfamiliar market.
3. Do you know the best market—worldwide—for your product?
4. This (product, service, etc.) will help you stay ahead of your (Japanese, German, etc.) competitors.
5. If you order now, it can be shipped immediately with another partial container load.
6. We can guarantee this price for six months even if currency changes force the dollar up.
7. There's a shortage of this product worldwide, but I can try to get you a (gross, ton, etc.); may I telex my home office to check?
8. Do you need the product in metric or American sizes?
9. Would you like us to bill you in your own currency to save exchange problems?
10. Do you have the power to commit your distributors worldwide to these products?

11. If you place this order through our (London, Paris, etc.) office, the EEC customs rate will lower your cost.
12. How would you like these shipped—by sea or air?
13. Do you believe that this model is best for (German, British, etc.) use?
14. We'll send an instructor who can speak (French, German, Arabic, etc.) and can teach your people how to operate the machines.
15. This will be the last shipment at these low costs; sea freight rates are going up 40 percent next month.
16. These products are really an insurance policy in case of international problems, since there's no domestic supplier.
17. This model was designed to meet (British, French, etc.) safety regulations.
18. We'll help you put together an advertisement that works well internationally when you use our magazine.
19. If you need shipment now, we can give it immediately; as you know, most European suppliers are closed for the month-long summer holiday.
20. This is the same model that your Japanese competitors use.
21. You're making the right decision. This is the best unit made for the (British, French, etc.) market.
22. With the labor union wage hikes you've faced in (Britain, Sweden, etc.), this automated machine can save you money.
23. We want to test a machine for (British, French, etc.) standards. Would you like to try it free for 60 days?
24. You've invested a lot in establishing a worldwide distributor network; now give them products that are easiest to sell.
25. Let us help you export with our know-how in the top markets globally.
26. Have you ever compared the cost of our product with that of the domestically produced product you are using now?
27. Would you like us to help arrange financing through an international bank?

Fifty Closing Lines That Work Internationally

28. The cost of this product is less than the cost of business lost from using this outdated (British, Japanese, etc.) product.
29. Make your new corporate management in (the United States, Germany, etc.) aware of your knowledge by recommending our service.
30. How do you know your (British, French, etc.) supplier is giving you the best possible service now?
31. We guarantee product satisfaction to you in any country.
32. Considering the current global shortage of (copper, oil, etc.), you're getting a real bargain.
33. Our distribution system reaches every country where you have plants.
34. The instructions for this product are printed in five languages, including (Arabic, German, etc.).
35. You've bought our service, so we'll offer your subsidiary companies the same service for half the price.
36. Let us do a "did-you-buy" study to determine how this service affected your export sales.
37. Do you know which export markets would be best for you?
38. Do you prefer our British or our French (jams, sweaters, etc.)?
39. Would you rather pay in British pounds or U.S. dollars?
40. Are you fully convinced that this product can help your export sales?
41. Once you sign this order, we'll serve as your overseas shipping consultant—free.
42. We'll be pleased to accept your (oil, coal, etc.) in payment for these goods.
43. If you order through our (London, Paris, etc.) office, it will provide a real tax advantage.
44. I have just one distributor—in France—with that product. Would you like me to reserve a unit for you?
45. With a lower inflation rate in Germany, we're able to keep your prices low.

46. Don't you agree that this convertible 110-220 V model is best for international use?
47. Only a German firm could give you a model of equal quality, but their price would be much higher due to the deutsche mark strength.
48. You can start with the basic set and be sure that you can add to it anywhere in the world.
49. Why wait, when global inflation is forcing prices up everywhere?
50. Someone with your taste for European styles should own this (car, dress, etc.). I'll make you a good price on it.

APPENDIX **A**

Some typical sales letters that help you close sales

#1 _____

HERE'S HOW JUST ONE AD CAN HELP YOU BEAT THE RECESSION!

If your sales need a boost, take some funds you've scheduled elsewhere and buy just *one* ad—in the first-ever U.S. Technology Supplement, to appear in the next issue of *Mining Equipment International*. Here's how it will help you:

1. It helps you take advantage of the depleted U.S. dollar—that inflation-shrunken dollar makes you more competitive in foreign markets today!
2. It helps you sell to the foreign markets that *are* strong and growing!
3. It lets you tie into MEI's U.S. Technology Supplement—to tell buyers worldwide about the advantages of U.S.-made equipment.

Just *one* ad will help you boost your sales and beat recession-related sales problems. To be part of this important supplement, call me or your sales representative.

#2 _____

Thank you for your letter dated May 19, 1980.

I take pleasure in enclosing full details for *Mining Equipment International*, together with a recent issue. In response to your question on preferred formats for new product announcements, I would recommend that you consider running a series of half-page advertisements.

The half-page size would allow you to fully inform our readers of your new product and would be placed adjacent to editorial matter. An example of this can be found on page 44 of the enclosed March issue.

The next available issue of *Mining Equipment International* is July/August, and we would be delighted to include your company within its pages.

Thank you for your interest.

#3 _____

Following our telephone conversation, I am happy to enclose a full media kit for *Mining Equipment International*, which includes our first Business Publications Audit statement.

As you will see, *Mining Equipment International* now shows a 91.4 percent individually requested circulation, of which just under 70 percent qualifies within one year. It is the only international mining magazine to cover both the coal and hard rock industry and does so at the lowest cost.

Naturally, we would be happy to include your company's equipment within the pages of *Mining Equipment International*, and I look forward to meeting you for further discussion before long.

#4 _____

Further to my telephone call to you today, I take pleasure in enclosing a copy of the June 10 *Business Opportunities Newsletter*, which contains some sales leads that might be of potential value. In particular, I refer to the call from Burma for various

Appendix A

pumps, the call for tenders from Egypt for irrigation pumps, and the Tanzanian reference to the need for ten water pumps (mobile).

This newsletter is part of the *World Construction* service to its advertisers and is sent as a separate air-mailed letter every month free of charge to advertisers using our magazine.

I am deliberately not introducing any form of World Construction sales promotion into this letter, because, as you are probably aware, I am already in close contact with your advertising agents, who represent you excellently in matters of media selection.

Incidentally, this *Business Opportunities Newsletter* is compiled from information sent to us regularly under contract by correspondents from the *Financial Times* situated in 76 countries throughout the world—a service that I believe to be exclusive to *World Construction* as the premier magazine in the international field of construction.

If you feel that I or my colleagues can be of any further service in this direction, please do not hesitate to call.

#5 _____

Re: October Supplement

Further to our telephone conversation yesterday, enclosed is a recent copy of *Mining Equipment International*, plus the circulation document.

I was pleased to hear that your company will participate in this special supplement in mining. So that you may decide which size advertisement you want to use, I am supplying the following details:

1. A4 page (e.g., pages 25 and 29) $1,170
2. 2/3 page (e.g., page 48) $ 710
3. ½ page (e.g., page 43) $ 560

As discussed, if we receive the official order and advertisement copy from your office, a 15 percent agency commission will be deducted from the gross billing.

I look forward to receiving confirmation of your advertising order for the October supplement, and should you need any further details, please do not hesitate to contact me.

#6 _____

Enclosed is a complete media package on *Mining Equipment International*. Please note the 1981 editorial calendar.

From our last conversation, I know you are close to finalizing your plan for 1981.

Although you are probably aware of this, I'd like to remind you that we ran a catalog release for you in the April issue of *Mining Equipment International*. That release generated 11 inquiries. Our regular advertisers with products similar to yours generate anywhere from 4 to 17 inquiries per issue. Further, by keeping the name of your company in front of our readership, you can establish a significant presence in the world mining community.

Therefore, when you consider your final budget for the remainder of this year and for 1981, please plan to use *Mining Equipment International*.

#7 _____

Thank you for our recent meeting when I had the opportunity to discuss *Mining Equipment International* and its potential in

Appendix A

promoting your clients in the global mining industry. Used as a major part of your clients' international advertising campaign, *Mining Equipment International* can provide many benefits.

Cost and circulation comparisons between *Mining Equipment International* and other journals in the field illustrate the reasons it would be logical to select our publication. *Mining Equipment International* is distinguished as the most efficient and economical publication to reach 15,500 key mining managers and engineers around the world, who are of prime purchasing influence.

The enclosed cost comparison chart emphasizes the cost efficiency of *Mining Equipment International*, when compared to journals of similar circulation, such as *World Mining*. *Mining Equipment International* will provide a 45 percent savings in cost, which is certainly an enlightening factor, especially when advertising funds are limited.

Editorially, *Mining Equipment International* is the only magazine that concentrates its reporting on the equipment being utilized in mining, thus creating the optimum environment for equipment advertisers such as your clients. Because of its format, *Mining Equipment International* provides all advertising campaigns with the maximum space to create the maximum impact. Even more significant: all advertising is positioned among informative editorial matter, thus assuring extra readability of your client's sales message.

Therefore, based on our professional circulation, solid publishing practices, and enlightening business economics, may we welcome you into the pages of *Mining Equipment International*, commencing with the April issue.

Once again, thank you for your courtesy. I look forward to developing a satisfying business relationship between our two companies.

#8 _____

I enjoyed having the opportunity of meeting you on Monday last and was most appreciative of your courtesy in letting me take up so much of your time to discuss *World Construction*. With the cooperation of your colleagues in the marketing department, I was able to leave with quite a lot of material from which we shall be able to prepare some editorial for inclusion in the August issue of *World Construction*. Furthermore, I hope that we shall be able to pursue the other idea that I put to you—the possibility of publishing an article that could form the basis of guideline instructions for contractors (especially in third world areas) for the preparation of construction sites pending the arrival of the building system. I think this would provide very worthwhile editorial and be of great value to your company as well.

I think I made it amply clear in my discussions with yourself and all your colleagues at your firm that it is not the policy of our company to make editorial in any way dependent on advertising support. The foremost consideration of any editorial feature must be its viability, determined solely by its readership interest. Having said that, however, I would be failing in my duty were I not to underline the obvious advantages to your company of advertising in *World Construction*. This is by any criteria the premier magazine in the international construction field. It has a wider circulation, carries more editorial features and more advertising, and has a better update of its recipients' qualifications and job functions than any other magazine in the field. This together with many other factors is a direct result of our being part of the Dun & Bradstreet organization.

But it is not my intention that this should be in any way a sales letter. I am just getting overly enthusiastic about the quality of our magazine. The object of this letter is to thank you for your courtesy and time and to express the hope that we will see each other again before long.

APPENDIX B

Some typical follow-up sales letters aimed at closing

#1 ──────────────────────

It was a pleasure to meet you once again at the coal show in Chicago.

Your positive reaction to the ore transport and handling feature appearing in the July/August issue of *Mining Equipment International* was greatly appreciated. Following further discussion with Ruth, I have held the multilingual oversize page facing this article open for your firm. If you wish to confirm this position, or perhaps acquire another position, just let me know.

Thanks once again for your time.

#2 ──────────────────────

I was very pleased to meet you once again in Chicago.

Following our conversation, I confirm that the July/August issue of *Mining Equipment International* will include a U.S. supplement. Through a combination of editorial and advertising, *Mining Equipment International* will inform readers of the technical advances American mining equipment manufacturers have been making and their ability to meet the needs of the worldwide mining industry.

This supplement will have separate covers, and we would like to offer your firm the inside front cover position at the regular rates. If you would like this, or another special position, then please just let me know.

#3 _____

Thank you for the courteous welcome you gave me when I visited your stand at Rockstore '80.

I also very much appreciate the time you spent with the European editor and me discussing your advertising objectives and *Mining Equipment International*.

I admire your honesty and forthright manner of expressing your dislike of the *Mining Equipment International* format. I also sincerely regret my inability to express my thoughts in German, since I have perceived from our short time together that I would enjoy the intellectual challenge of debating the subject with you. Suffice it to say that there are some disadvantages in the format. But all products, even those of Westfalia Lunen, have advantages and disadvantages. Like the advantages of all Westfalia Lunen products, the many advantages of the *Mining Equipment International* format outweigh the few disadvantages. And most importantly, after only two years on the market, 70 percent of the 15,500 mining engineers who receive the publication are *personally* requesting us to send it to them. I respectfully submit to you that this is the most serious expression of acceptance of the format and the contents.

With the resources and expertise of your department, the cost of producing an effective advertisement to test the value of *Mining Equipment International* and its size would not be an impossible one. A four-color full-page advertisement appearing six times would cost only DM 22,410, a fraction of the cost of a program of inserts, such as you now use in other magazines. As a result, you would have an excellent exposure and an excellent volume of replies.

In closing, please allow me to express my sincere appreciation for the small campaign you ran in *Mining Equipment International* to support your presence at the coal show in Chicago. Thank you also for considering the possibility of a more effective and serious business cooperation.

#4 ─────────────────────────────────

I was very grateful for your courtesy in letting me discuss *World Construction* and what it has to offer when I came to your offices last Monday. I felt that you gave a very warm and sympathetic consideration to my presentation, and this has encouraged me to write to you now and strongly reurge that, even though it may not be possible at this time for your company to place a complete schedule of advertising, it would be very advantageous to the promotion of your overseas sales if you were to be featured in the advertising pages of our August issue. You will recall, no doubt, that we are running a special feature on low-cost building and building systems. We are featuring your product in the editorial of that issue, but it would obviously carry more impact if it were substantiated by display advertising. This would give significant impetus to your own salesmen's approaches to their individual plans. The prestige accruing from representation in a magazine such as *World Construction* is of great effect.

Once again, thank you for receiving me.

#5 ─────────────────────────────────

Many thanks for your time and hospitality when we recently discussed the potential of *Mining Equipment International* in your company's international communications program.

Your favorable evaluation of *Mining Equipment International* was appreciated, especially since it is distinguished as the most *efficient and cost-effective* mining publication to reach 15,500 key mining managers and engineers globally. I was pleased to hear that you plan to utilize *Mining Equipment International* in your future advertising, and as discussed, I would recommend that you book your advertising schedule prior to May 31 to secure full rate protection, thus avoiding the forthcoming 15 percent rate increase.

Once again, Mr. XYZ, thank you for your courtesy, and I look forward to the development of a rewarding business relationship between our two companies.

#6 _____

Many thanks for your time recently and your excellent company at an enjoyable dinner. I found it most interesting and informative to hear about your company's international marketing activities.

In reference to *Mining Equipment International* I appreciated your favorable evaluation, especially since it is distinguished as the most *efficient and cost-effective* publication to reach 15,500 key mining managers and engineers who are of major purchasing influence around the world.

Further to our discussions, I am pleased to confirm that the October issue will feature a preview of Fetex '80 and the November/December issue will include a U.K. supplement, which editorially will promote your international sales message. The closing date for advertising copy for the November/December issue is October 12; I look forward to receiving confirmation of your advertising plans.

I would like to point out that, as with all marketing activities, continuity is an important factor. Therefore, I would recom-

Appendix B

mend that you consider planning an advertising series in *Mining Equipment International* to create maximum impact, especially for the extensive interest you have in the forthcoming Haroogate exhibition and long-term export activities.

Once again, John, thank you for your courtesy. I look forward to the development of a rewarding business relationship between our two companies.

In the meanwhile, should you require any further information, please do not hesitate to contact me.

#7 ───────────────────────────────

Thank you for letting me take your time this morning to explain the benefits of *World Construction*. I am enclosing an additional copy of the January issue and the tear sheet requested for your photographer when we featured your firm on the front cover.

I am also enclosing some media details, including a photocopy of the "did-you-buy" letter that I explained to you.

If you examine the enclosed BPA circulation statement (which, incidentally, constitutes a formal legal document backed by the Dun & Bradstreet reputation), you cannot fail to be impressed by the precise statement of readership and areas of circulation.

You will appreciate too that we are the only magazine in the field that can claim a 100 percent total qualified circulation. Of the 28,564 total, 99.8 percent (28,509) of the copies are sent in response to personally written requests from readers defined by name and job function. Furthermore, we are unique in being able to claim that 84.8 percent of the circulation are qualified within one year. The remaining 15.2 percent are qualified on a two-year basis. In other words, we are giving you an exact legalized breakdown of circulation that is precise in definition of recipients and areas that cannot be equaled by any other magazine using the ABC-type audit. In addition to this, the superiority of the technical information contained in the editorial articles in *World Construction* is self-evident when compared with other magazines in the field.

I am sure your sales force would benefit from the backup they would get from your advertising in *World Construction* and *Mining Equipment International*.

#8 _____

Many thanks for taking the time recently to discuss the potential of using *Mining Equipment International* in your client's international communications program.

Your favorable evaluation of *Mining Equipment International* was appreciated, especially since it is distinguished as the most *efficient and cost-effective* publication to reach 15,500 key mining personnel who are of major purchasing influence around the world.

As I understand from our meeting, your client's schedules are planned for 1980. I would however recommend serious consideration for the November/December issue, which features both a U.K. supplement and a special article on "Drilling and Blasting." Copy deadline is October 12.

Once again thank you for your courtesy, and I hope that *Mining Equipment International* can be of service in promoting your client's future international sales message.

Should you require any further information, please do not hesitate to contact us.

#9 _____

Thanks for visiting with me during my recent trip to Salt Lake City.

On the basis of our discussion, I think it makes sense to take an umbrella contract for nine pages and split them between process machinery and the mining division.

Please note that *Mining Equipment International* is an equipment-oriented publication. In 1979 we ran 18 articles devoted specifically to processing and 26 articles devoted exclusively to transportation equipment. We are now producing qualified leads for your competitors.

We are anticipating a rate increase in 1981. Orders for 1981 business received prior to October 15, 1980 will enjoy rate protection throughout the contract period.

#10 ───────────────────────────────────────

Thank you very much for allowing me to present *Mining Equipment International* to you yesterday.

Please find enclosed a copy of the article that appeared in the July/August 1979 issue of *Mining Equipment International* and resulted in 147 sales leads for your client.

If you require any further information at this point, please contact me.

Index

accounting servicing
   as element of follow-up selling, 69
   use of, 73–74
advantages, buyer, listing
   example of, 85
   as prerequisite to sales calls, 85
advertising, as initial means of selling, 52
advice, offering, to hold buyer's attention, 32–33
aggressiveness, buyer dissatisfaction with, 41
ambition
   as qualification for salespersons, 79–80
   as motivating factor, 80
American Express, marketing services giveaways of, 56
anecdotes
   as aid for holding buyer's attention, 27
   as nonstop selling technique, 59
   use of, for buyer's identifiability with product, 40
"asking for orders"
   importance of, 86
   as selling rule, 70
assurance, offering, as nonstop selling technique, 63–64

attainability of goals, 80–82
attention, buyer's, holding
   importance of, 24
   ineffectiveness of gimmicks in, 24–25
   through interruptions, 27–29
   through product information, 29–30
   through product pricing, 30–31
   show and tell for, 33, 35
   through understanding buyer's needs, 24–25
   using advice for, 32–33
audiovisual aids, use of, 33

balance sheet, 33
benefits, product, relating, to buyers, 37
brevity of presentation, 29
budgets, limited
   as buyer objection, 60
   handling buyer's, 60–61
buyers
   attention of, *see* attention, buyer's, holding
   dissatisfaction of, 41
   group, 11
   identifiability of, with product, 40
   motivating, 59, 70

buyers (*continued*)
  needs of, *see* needs, buyer
  objections of, 46, 60–61
  personality preference of, 69
buying decisions, negative, 19
buying patterns, 14

call reports
  examples of, 87–90, 90–91
  use of, 86, 90, 94
call scheduling
  instructing, 83, 85–86
  worksheet for, 84
clients, long-standing
  follow-up selling to, 69
  see also buyers
closing
  block, 104–106
  on implied consent, 71
  importance of listening in, *see* listening
  instructing, *see* instructing salespersons
  lines, *see* closing lines
  manager's role in, *see* managers, sales
  price negotiations for, *see* price negotiations
  product options for, *see* options, product
  selling techniques for, *see* follow-up selling; give-to-get selling, nonstop selling; self-selling, telephone selling
  use of discounts for, 44–45
  use of joint calls for, *see* joint calls
  see also attention, buyer's, holding, buyers; presentations, sales; products; questions; salespersons; selling

closing lines
  for industrial selling, 118–121
  for intangibles, 123–128
  for international sales, 129–132
  for retail selling, 115–117
  for wholesale sales, 122–124
competition
  use of, to hold buyer's attention, 31–32
con artists, 4–5
confidence, gaining, as element of repeat sales, 74
consideration, importance of, 70
consultant, role of, in follow-up selling, 73
controversy, avoiding, 29–30
corporate nonstop selling, 65–66, 68
cyclical buying pattern, 14

dialogue, sales call, 96
"did you buy" study, as give-to-get selling technique, 54, 56
discounts
  fairness of, 44–45
  interest rates as determining, 45
  invoice payments for, 45
  old accounts and, 21
  use of, for closing sales, 45
dismissals of salespersons, 111

economic conditions, use of, to create product interest, 29
emotional appeal
  to motivate buyers, 70
  as nonstop selling technique, 59
estimate form, monthly, 90
  exampe of, 91
  use of, 90
experimental product, price negotiating for, 51–52

Index

fear of salespeople, 18
flip chart, use of, in sales presentations, 85
follow-through, importance of, 41
follow-up letters
  examples of, 139–145
  use of, 72
follow-up selling
  accounting services as, 73–74
  closing sales through, 71–72
  elements in, 69
  letters for, 139–145
  listening to close, 11, 16
  long-standing clients and, 69
  nonstop selling for, 62–63
  recording buyer information for, 14, 42
  repeat sales as type of, 69
  technique of, 69–71
franchises, product modification in, 42–43
free services, price negotiating through, 46–49
frequency discounts, 21
future sales, *see* follow-up selling

"get acquainted" call, 39
gimmicks
  giveaway, *see* giveaways
  use of, to hold buyer's attention, 24–25
  use of, to instruct salespersons, 106–107
giveaways
  marketing services as, 56
  avoidance of, in sales, 57–58
  see also give-to-get selling
give-to-get selling
  adapting techniques of, 56–57
  price negotiating through, 48–49

rules as problem of, 57–58
as technique for closing sales, 53–56
see also giveaways
goals, establishing, of salespersons, 80–82
good–guy/bad–guy routines, as gimmick for training salespersons, 107
group, buying, 11
group selling, price negotiating for, 50–51

humanizing selling, through giveaways, 56–57

illustrations, use of, in follow-through selling, 41
imagination, use of, to hold buyer's attention, 27
insights, 9–10
intangibles, selling, 38–39
interest rates, effect of, on discounts, 45
internal corporate nonstop selling, 65–66, 68
interruptions, restoring sales presentations after, 27–29
investment, 41
item-by-item presentation, use of, to overcome price resistance, 46

joint calls
  evaluating sales training through, 103
  evaluation form for, 101
  as instructional technique, 99–103
  use of, to remedy closing difficulties, 105–106

Judith Sans International
  as example of group selling, 50
  as example of product modification, 42

"leave-behinds," 33, 35
letters
  follow-up, 72, 139–145
  handwritten, as aid for holding buyer's attention, 27
  sales, *see* letters, sales
letters, sales
  examples of, 133–138
  guidelines for writing, 94
  instructing salespersons in writing, 94
  use of, to supplement personal visits, 60
listening
  as aid in dealing with buyer objections, 60–61
  customer record cards and, 12–14
  gaining insights through, 9, 11
  as guide to sales presentation, 18
  habits, developing, 22–23
  importance of, for price negotiating, 49
  importance of, for telephone sales calls, 17–18
  learning buyer needs through, 21–22
  reinforcing, 11, 14, 16
  use of, for self-selling, 16–17
literature, use of, to hold buyer's attention, 33
locale of presentation, selection of, 28
long-standing clients, selling to, 69

managers, sales
  role of, in joint calls, 104
  training of salespersons by, *see* training salespersons
marketing services
  as giveaways, 56
  as give-to-get selling technique, 54
medium-term goals, 80–81
Million Dollar Roundtable, 77
modification, product, *see* product modification
monthly estimate form, 90, 94
motivation
  buyer, appealing to, 70
  as changing with the times, 70
  salesperson's, 80

needs, buyer
  concern for, displaying, 16–17
  establishing, through listening, 21–22
  follow-through and, 41
  holding buyer attention through knowledge of, 25–26, 29, 30
  listing, in sales priority chart, 14–16
  product modification to satisfy, 36–37
  tailoring questions to, 9–10
negative buying decisions, 19
negative selling, avoidance of, 31–32
nonstop selling
  assurance as technique of, 63–64
  importance of, for continuing sales, 62
  internal corporate, 65–66
  overselling in, avoidance of, 64–65

Index

problems faced during, 60–61
  results of, 66, 68
  role reversal as aid in, 61–62
    results of, 66, 68
  techniques for, 59–60
notes, use of
  in holding buyer's attention, 26
  in selling, 19–20

objections, buyer
  dealing with, 60–61
  as problem of nonstop selling, 60
objections, product, overcoming, 109–110
options, product
  buyer identifiability with, 40
  buyer selection of, 38–39
  follow-through on, 41
  new options for, provision of, 42–43
  sales through 39–40
  use of, to satisfy buyer needs, 36–37
order pad, 26
overselling
  avoiding, 64–65
  vs. nonstop selling, 65

payments, budget, to overcome price resistance, 46
payments, monthly, to overcome price resistance, 46
paper-and-pencil method of holding buyer's attention, 33–34
performance, salesperson's, 94, 95
persistence, as technique in follow-up selling, 70
personal services, use of, in give-to-get selling, 54, 56–67
persuasion, 9

plus-and-minus ledger
  example of, 34
  use of, 33, 35
presentations, sales
  "asking for orders" during, 70, 86
  buyer's attention during, *see* buyer's attention, holding
  closing, *see* closing
  controversy during, avoiding, 29–30
  interruptions during, 27–29
  item-by-item, 46
  leave-behinds for, 33, 35
  length of, 29
  location of, 28
  modifying, to suit buyer's needs, 18, 41
  prerequisite for, 85, 86
  rehearsing, 85, 86
  use of flipchart in, 85
  use of videotape in, 85
  see also selling
price negotiating
  through discounting, 21, 44–45
  group, 50–51
  importance of listening in, 49
  through offering of free services, 47–49
  overcoming price resistance through, 45–47
  in unestablished price structures, 51–52
  word cues to begin, 47
  see also pricing
pricing
  holding buyer's attention by, 30–31
  resistance to, 45
  service, 45–46

pricing (*continued*)
  see also price negotiating
product(s)
  benefits, relating, to buyer's needs, 37
  experimental, price negotiating for, 51–52
  information, 29–30
  interest, generating, through economic conditions, 29
  modification of, *see* product modification
  new, *see* product(s), new
  objections to, overcoming, 109–110
  options, *see* options, product
  pricing, *see* price negotiating
product(s), new
  price negotiating for, 51–52
  reliability of, importance of developing, 29
product modification
  need for, 36–37
  providing new options through, 42–43
  use of psychology in, 38
promotional mailings, use of, to supplement personal visits, 60
prospect cards
  example of, 94–95
  use of, 90
prospecting, instructing, to salespersons, 83
psychology, use of, in product modification, 38

qualifications, salesperson's, 79–80
questions
  holding buyer's attention by, 29
  phrasing, 10–11

  self-selling through, 16–17
  tailoring, to buyer's needs, 9–10
  use of, for future sales, 14, 16

reason, as means of motivating buyers, 70
record cards, customer
  examples of, 12–13
  use of, 14
references, use of, for buyer assurance, 63
refresher course, use of, 106
rehearsals of sales presentations, 85, 86
relationships, sales, 71
repeat sales, *see* follow-up selling
repetition, as nonstop selling technique, 59
relating to buyers, 26
report, call, *see* call report
resistance, 46
role playing
  as instructional technique, 98, 99
  use of tape recorders for, 107
rules, modification of, in give-to-get selling, 57–58

sales call dialogue, 96
salespersons
  buyer's fear of, 18
  dismissal of, 111
  goals of, 80–82
  motivating, 80
  qualifications of, 79–80
  trainability of, 78
  training, *see* training salespersons
sales priority chart
  example of, 15
  use of, 14–16

Index

sales relationships, 71
sales volume, use of, as indicator of closing failures, 106
satisfaction selling, 26
   through product options, 37, 40
   as tool for follow-up selling, 73
scheduling, call, *see* call scheduling
seasonal buying pattern, 14
self-confidence, displaying, as technique in follow-up selling, 70
self-selling
  in follow-up selling, 70
  listening as aiding, 16–17
selling
  as an art, 3–4
  corporate, 65–66, 68
  follow-up, *see* follow-up selling
  give-to-get, *see* give-to-get selling
  group, 50–51
  humanizing, 56–57
  importance of listening in, *see* listening
  intangibles, 38–39
  negative, 31–32
  nonstop, *see* nonstop selling
  over-, 64–65
  through product options, 39–40
  repeat, *see* follow-up selling
  satisfaction, 26, 37, 40, 73
  self-, *see* self-selling
  specialty, 25
  statistics on, 59
  telephone, *see* telephone selling
  tools, 39, 40, 48
service pricing, as method of discounting, 45–46
servicing, *see* account servicing; marketing services
short-term goals, 80–81
sincerity
  as technique in follow-up selling, 70
  importance of, 63
smiling, 69
specialty selling, 25

tape recording, as aid in salesperson's instruction, 106–107
telephone selling
  importance of listening in, 17–18
  in supplementing personal visits, 60
  use of sales priority chart for, 16
testimonials, use of, for holding buyer's attention, 27
time
  importance of managing, in selling, 70
  as investment in nonstop selling, 64
trade shows, 65
trainability, determining salesperson's, 78
training curriculum, 95, 97
training salespersons
  in call scheduling, 83–84, 85
  in closing, 98–103
  curriculum for, 95–97
  good-guy/bad-guy routine for, 107
  through joint calls, 99–103, 105–106
  in letter writing, 94
  measuring ability of, 78–80
  in overcoming objections to products, 109–110

training salesperson (*continued*)
  performance evaluation as element of, 94–95
  in planning sales, 82–85
  in prospecting, 83, 86, 90, 94
  rehearsals as method for, 85, 86
  through role playing, 98–99
  in sales presentations, 85, 86
trouble shooting, accounting services handling of, 73

videotape, use of, 85

visits
  as follow-up selling technique, 73–74
  supplementing, through promotional mailing, 60
volume, sales, as determinant of closing failure, 106
volume discounts, 21

you, use of
  in follow-up selling, 70
  in sales presentations, 17, 26